"Living in Two Worlds: Destined f[...] Allen is an honest read. In this book, the author becomes a poster model of a "Before and After" image. The book documents the journey of an individual who illustrates that no matter where you start in life, with the help and guidance of God, you can make it as far as you choose to progress! Kimberly's "Before" was challenged with an environment that was not conducive to growth and achievement, but when she was blessed to surround herself with a powerful, positive, and productive atmosphere, Kimberly's "After" flourished to amazing heights like a flower that keeps on peaking and blooming day in and day out! Kimberly's "After" is detailed in the scriptures - Proverbs 31:1 "Who can find a virtuous woman? For her price is far above rubies." This book is a must read for anyone who needs encouragement to keep pressing toward the mark that they are destined to reach.

Pastor Jonathan W. Allen, Sr.
Connect Church
Waldorf, Maryland

"Everybody has a story to tell. Some are more dramatic than others, and some are more compelling than others! This book is the story of survival amidst overwhelming oppressive odds. A single mother with a boyfriend who is a major drug dealer is the stuff of movies and fairy tales. Yet, Kim Allen, has not only survived that lifestyle but also is alive to tell of her harrowing experience of promiscuous sex, drug trafficking , and raising a son in a patently dysfunctional environment; this indeed is a riveting story. It is really the story of how God's providence can work through the most gut-wrenching situations! Like the story of Jabaz in 1 Chronicles

4:9-10, Kim was more honorable, and God heard her pray for something better, something with eternal consequences, and something that would touch the lives of many. This is a must read story that will take you on a journey of pain, suffering, misunderstandings, and discovery of the tenacious love of God!

Dr. James Love

LIVING IN

Two
WORLDS
DESTINED FOR CHANGE

Dedication and Acknowledgments

Iwant to dedicate this book to my husband Jonathan, my angel, who has been loving, amazing, and supportive. You stuck with me through it all, and I appreciate you for loving me even when I made it difficult. I also want to dedicate this book to my sons, James and Jonathan, Jr., and my grandchildren, Jaquan and Iyana. As you continue to move in your life's purpose, don't stop dreaming and live life to the fullest. You all are my greatest life support, and I love us!

Writing this book was a struggle from the beginning, and I didn't understand why God had me write it until I realized that it wasn't about me but about the reader. Don't get me wrong; I am grateful to my Heavenly Father for allowing me to write this book now, and I'm hopeful that a change will take place in the life of each reader.

I have to acknowledge my husband Jonathan again because he's been nothing short of supportive for thirty-eight years. He has believed in me since our first encounter in April 1981. Whatever I desired to do in life, he pushed me and supported me every step of the way.

I would also like to acknowledge Dr. James Love and Mrs. Bertha Thomas for taking time out of their busy lives to read my manuscript and help make this book become reality.

Thank you to Wendi Hayman of Glory to Glory Publications, LLC; God allowed us to meet, and I'm so thankful.

Last, but not least, I have to acknowledge my parents Carl S. Reeder and Ruby Reeder. I couldn't write this book without them because they are the reason it was written. I am also grateful for all of my siblings sticking together as a family through the tough times.

To all others who have impacted my life, thank you for what you have given me.

Introduction

Change from the Inside Out

Dear God,

I pray to You this morning asking You to lead me in the direction You would have me to go. I'm up this morning at 6:05 a.m. believing that I'm supposed to start journaling so I can begin writing the book You placed inside of me. Please help me dear Lord and show me where to begin!

Oftentimes, when people set out to change their lives after life-altering events, they start with a change that others can see. They change their hair with a haircut, color, or new style, or they change their style of dress. They even change their weight by drastically gaining or losing weight. Although the changes people make to their outer appearances will get them the applause of man, these changes will not bring them long-lasting results that are essential for proper mental and emotional healing. It's the change to the mind and heart that brings the long-lasting results necessary to live a viable and productive life past the hurt we've experienced. We have to uproot a lot of the seeds that were planted in us during our childhood because those have the most impact on the decisions we make in life, how we choose to live our lives, and which relationships we pursue.

Romans 12:2 (NLT) says, "Don't copy the behavior and customs of this world, but let God transform you into a new person by changing the way you think. Then you will learn to know God's will for you, which is good and pleasing and perfect." Typically when we think of transformation, we use the example of a caterpillar transforming into a butterfly, but that only illustrates outer transformation. Scripture tells us that transformation takes place by renewing the mind. The mind must be changed from the old way of thinking, which is learned by what we see and experience in life.

Transformation is not a one-time occurrence like the caterpillar transforming into a butterfly. We have to transform our minds continually because as we go through life, we will always face people, situations, and circumstances that will impact us in some way. In order for those past occurrences to not impair us, we have to renew our minds so that we're able to live fruitfully and be "good and pleasing and perfect" according to the will of God. We cannot allow anything that has happened to us to affect us long-term, mentally or emotionally. We have to get to a place where we're able to still give God glory, honor, and praise with our lives.

This is my story of how God transformed me from the inside out because I was *Destined for Change*. I have written it with the express purpose of helping young women cope with the issues they may face daily. Some young ladies chase after love and attention due to rejection and abandonment issues, and they turn to the world to fill that need through illicit sex, underage drinking, and illegal drugs. My prayer is that by me being open and honest about the things I did in my youth, I can minister to those who may have succumbed to the same destructive lifestyle I once lived so that they can see that God can and will help them escape, just as He helped me.

God can and will change you when you allow Him to do

so. He did it for me once I gave my total heart to him. Please open your heart to receive God's love. Know that I'm praying for you as you read through my dramatic and often painful life story. Believe me when I say God is faithful!

This is a faithful saying:
For if we died with Him,
We shall also live with Him.
If we endure,
We shall also reign with Him.
If we deny Him,
He also will deny us.
If we are faithless,
He remains faithful;
He cannot deny Himself.
(2 Timothy 2:11-13 NKJV)

1

Special Little Niece

I grew up in a large family of eight children: Annie, Carol, Sylvia, Carl, Jr., Jimmie, Winifred (Wendy), Anthony, and me. I was the second to the youngest and the youngest of the five girls. Growing up in a family of eight kids, it was hard to get special attention from my parents, especially when they were dealing with the dysfunction of their marriage. However, I was destined to be different from my siblings even from birth. The choices I made in life, good and bad, set me apart from everyone else. As I look back on it, I was the one in my family who was chosen for God's purpose to prevail in the earth through the Reeder family.

When I think back to what I know of the beginning of my life, it reminds me of Mary and Joseph trying to find somewhere for Mary to give birth to Jesus (Luke 2:7). As my dad tells the story, I was born on the floor of the emergency room at Washington Hospital Center. Since my mother didn't get prenatal care while she was carrying me, the hospital staff didn't allow her to go into the maternity unit with the other mothers because they thought she might've been carrying some type of disease. There was no place for me at the "inn" so to speak. The strange beginnings of my life didn't end on that emergency room floor. They continued with the wrong name and birth date being recorded on my birth record. As long as I can remember, I was Kimberly Yvette Reeder born July 18, 1960. Then, in my early forties, I discovered that the spelling of my name and the date recorded on my birth certificate were both wrong. The document says: Kimberely Yvett Reeder, date of birth July 19, 1960. My dad swears that I was born on July 18th and that the doctor who delivered me and filled out the birth certificate was drunk and recorded the information wrong.

I was also born with a speech impediment that I inherited from my father, so elementary school was a challenge for me. I was held back in the second grade because the school administration said I wasn't ready for the next grade level and suggested I go to a speech therapy class. Unfortunately, that turned out to be a traumatic experience for me. When I went to the speech therapy class for the first time, the teacher had me read something while she recorded me. Then, she played the recording so I could hear myself reading. My voice sounded like a voice from hell! I sounded like a monster to myself. It sounded so awful that I ran out of the class and never returned. After that incident, I developed a complex about my voice and withdrew from interacting much with others to avoid being teased about my deep, stuttering voice.

This speech impediment was passed down to my father from his mother, my grandma Charlotte, and was ultimately passed down to me and three of my brothers. I guess at home I didn't recognize that there was a problem with the way I talked because my father and brothers talked the same way.

It's crazy how we initially don't know that we have a deficiency until someone else points it out to us, and when they do, it changes our entire outlook on ourselves. That is why we have to be careful of what we allow others to say about us, especially as children. Later in my life when God called me to preach the gospel, like a foolish woman, I ran from it for ten years. For one thing, I could hardly speak three words without stuttering, and I wasn't about to try to preach to anybody with the way my voice sounds! I believe that had my speech impediment not been highlighted or magnified to me in that way when I was in elementary school, I would've made it through life just fine with how my voice sounded. I must say that it took a long time for me to be able to accept my voice as it is.

I've often wondered why I've inherited the majority of my physical traits from my father, and when I was young, I developed a complex about those traits and didn't like who I was. Along with his speech impediment, I inherited his big feet, skinny legs, height, and ashy, tough, dry skin. My sisters, who are all older than me, inherited my mother's average height, small feet, good speech, and nice legs. It just didn't seem fair to me that I got what I considered to be all of my father's negative attributes. It took me a very long time to stop comparing myself to my sisters and to be confident with myself. I have my mother's upper body and my father's lower body, and I've always felt like this was a freaky combination. However, I have learned to appreciate my body over the years and give God the glory for it.

When I was eight years old, my mother's uncle came to Washington, D.C. from South Carolina for a visit. Even though our house was already overcrowded with kids, my parents allowed him to stay with us while he was in the process of buying a dry cleaning business. I was smitten with my uncle; he was small in stature, very handsome, and had nice hair that always looked good, and he looked like he could've been in his mid-forties. My uncle wore dark glasses with gold rims and dressed sharply and neatly. He wore nice creased slacks, sweater-like shirts with collars, and shoes that were sleek looking with pointed toes and a high shine.

When I met my uncle's girlfriend, Ms. Rose, she was a nice petite woman who wore fancy cat-shaped eyeglasses. She was small in stature as well, and she was very stylish and wore beautiful clothes that I admired. Seeing her in her stylish clothing is one of the reasons why I love fashion and why I wanted to model and become a fashion designer. After a while, my uncle invited me to come along with him when he went to visit Ms. Rose, and they would take me with them to different places. She was one of the few people I believed really liked me. I remember one time when she bought me a beautiful light cream coat that I cherished until I grew out of it.

After my uncle purchased the dry cleaning business, he would bring me along to help him run it. I became my uncle's special little niece, not knowing what was in store for me. Later, he started offering me money to clean his room in our house and for helping him out at the cleaners. I liked having money of my own because with eight children in the family, there wasn't a lot of extra money, let alone enough to give out to us kids. We didn't have much as a family, and we didn't get treats and snacks often; so, I took the money I earned from my uncle and spent it at the corner store called Brown Street Market, which wasn't that far from my house.

After going through what I would say was him "baiting me in," which is known as grooming, my uncle later expanded my opportunities to make more money. Since I was enjoying having my own money, I was definitely excited to get more.

He started offering me money to allow him to touch me in my private place. My child mind didn't fully comprehend what he was asking of me, so I went along with what he asked and accepted the money every time he offered it. My uncle told me that I couldn't tell anyone about our special arrangement; he said it was only for me, his special niece. I liked being deemed his special niece and the money I got for it. This man who I admired and trusted took away my innocence when I was only eight years old!

Not too long after that, something happened in my uncle and Ms. Rose's relationship, and he returned to South Carolina. The sexual abuse I endured ended when he left, but the damage was done and impacted my life immensely down the road. I never shared what my uncle did to me with my parents or sisters until after I was grown and married. I was too ashamed to tell anyone. Over the years, I've had so many questions run through my mind: *What would people think of me if they knew? Did I like what happened to me? Would I have gotten in trouble if I told?* I didn't know what to do at such a young age. I wasn't sure if I liked what was happening to me or not. That was my biggest issue because I wasn't sure if I should've liked it or not, especially since I didn't know what it really was or what to do about it. I rationalized later that I must have liked it because as I grew older, in my mind, all I wanted to do was entertain a man whether it was topless or bottomless. If my parents had found out what my uncle did to me, I bet I would have gotten the worst whipping ever with the razor strap from my mother because it was her family member. I think my father wouldn't have looked at me in the same way, and then I wouldn't have had anyone to treat me special. For years, these were the thoughts that were in my mind. I had to get free from those thoughts that controlled me so that I could be free from the trauma of my past.

When parents invite family members and friends into their homes, they do so with a high level of trust because they, after all, are family. They don't suspect that a family member would do any harm or bring about any danger toward them and especially not toward their children. It's with great misfortune that this isn't always the case. Statistics show that 1 in 5 girls and 1 in 20 boys are victims of sexual abuse by a family member in the home (*victimsofabuse.org*), and sexual molestation was happening way more often in the 60s and 70s than it is nowadays. It's sad to say, but parents then were more focused on working hard to provide for their family or on having a good time to pay attention to their children and what was potentially happening to them. As tragic as it is, these types of experiences set children up for following some destructive paths later on in life, living a life of withdrawal from society, or being unable to trust those who are most important in their lives.

If you went through a traumatic childhood experience that has had an affect on your adult life, you can be set free from your past. Understand that what happened to you is not your fault. Release the guilt, anguish, and shame. The purpose for your life was established before you were born, and this is something that Satan knows. Therefore, what happened to you was an attack or attempt to derail and stop you from living out your purpose and God's will for your life so that you don't reach your destiny that was predestined before the foundation of the earth. Even if you've done some things in your past that were your fault, once you've repented and been forgiven, you can release that as well.

Talk about the experience, and absolutely don't keep it bottled up on the inside.

Think about Job when he was afflicted. He released all of his thoughts, feelings, anguish, and pain to his friends and to God. The release is necessary to clear space so your spirit can be open to receive everything you need to be healed, made whole, and at peace.

Get help and support from someone you trust: a family member, friend, or therapist. Help and support gives you the necessary encouragement and strength you need for the journey to freedom. There will be some aspects of the journey that you can handle alone, but not all. You're going to want to have someone standing alongside you who can lift you up at those moments of weakness so that you won't give up and can continue to press through. Know that you can be free and can rebuild your life beyond your past.

John 8:36 (NLT) says, "So if the Son sets you free, you are truly free," and this is God's promise for you and your freedom. Freedom from your past is available to you. Make the decision to choose freedom from the bondage of your past. Once you choose to be free, you can rebuild your life by changing the course or direction in which you were going to one that will lead you to your purpose and destiny. Choose to go in the opposite direction of the one you were going in when you were bound to your past. Choose to change the course of your thinking from thoughts relative to your past, and think thoughts that are positive and relative to your purposeful future. Make decisions and take actions based on the freedom you now live. Make small changes until your life is completely lived on the path of freedom.

2

Functioning in Dysfunction

Domestic violence along with child, mental, and alcohol abuse were all elements of my childhood. I definitely didn't grow up in the best environment, and unfortunately, it wasn't the most loving one either. My siblings and I were pretty much destined to become dysfunctional ourselves or end up having some form of destructive behavior. We were never told, "I love you," nor did we receive hugs growing up.

My dad was a functioning alcoholic and had his share of issues; although he worked every day and was a good provider for the family, he bullied my mother and his children. Nevertheless, I'm still grateful and thankful to the Lord for my family. My father would tell us how he had it rough when he was a child. That would be his explanation to us when he needed to justify why he was so abusive. He blamed everything on his horrible upbringing, slave mentality, and the punishments he received. He gave his eight children similar beatings like those he received and would justify it by saying, "I'm doing the best I know how to do as a father."

My father would always tell us about his rough upbringing. He would tell us about how he walked to school with holes in his shoes or about the bad things he and his brother used to do, like steal money from the church offering plate and hide it under the floorboard so they could later buy treats. When they got caught, they had to go to reform school, which was as bad as being at home.

My father grew up to be an angry man thanks to the treatment he received as a child. When he was angry, he'd pick up anything he could get his hands on and use it to beat my mother. We never knew what exactly caused my father to abuse my mother. We assumed it was because she wouldn't have sex with him, something wasn't done in the house that he thought needed to be done, she was too generous when she didn't have it to give, or she wouldn't discipline us when we needed it. As I recall, the worst times at home were after he had been drinking; that's when he would get extremely violent with her. My parents' bedroom door stayed closed most of the time, but we could still hear her crying and hollering. We used to bang on the door, screaming and crying, and beg our father to stop beating our mother. It was always hard to just sit and listen to the ruckus. The one thing we never understood was how she could be so nice to him later on or the next day. *How could she be so happy and content after she was beaten like a slave?*

We were always afraid of our father during his alcoholic outbursts, and we worried about what he would do to our mother. At times, we'd encourage her to take us, leave, and go back home to her family in South Carolina. She did try to leave a few times, but my father would always go south to get her. As soon as they were in the house, he would start beating her again. I'm not sure why she always came back, but I think my father probably threatened to hurt us if she didn't come back home.

Not long after we moved into our second house, when I was age 10, my parents got into a huge fight. This was the first time I'd actually seen my dad abuse my mother; I'd only heard it throughout the years. Hearing the stories from my older siblings, it seemed the abuse started when they were young kids.

My father was not the type of man to try and buck up against, period. My dad used to make whipping straps for belts at his job. Picture the straps barbers use to sharpen their blades and how thick they were. Well, my dad made some like those but just a little thinner and a little wider. He didn't play when it came down to whipping his kids. At times, I am told, he would beat my older siblings with iron cords, water hoses, and extension cords. Even though my whippings were few and far between, when I did get them, he used that strap and whipped me like a runaway slave. We would get whippings for any and everything we did wrong, including going to bed with one cup left in the sink, leaving the kitchen floor half done, peeling too much off the potatoes, standing with one foot on top of the other and messing up our shoes, having company on the front porch, or not washing our clothes at the scheduled time. Sometimes the punishment was mental abuse from his screaming and yelling at us or spewing obscenities and negativity at us. He also had creative punishments like making us stand in the middle of the floor holding a heavy wooden chair in each hand with our arms held up and one foot in the air; if we let one of our arms or legs drop before he instructed, we would get the worst beating. My two oldest siblings left home at fifteen and seventeen to escape the mental and physical abuse.

Even though our household was in turmoil for the most part, we had fun on the weekends when our parents would invite their friends and family over to play cards, drink, and smoke. They used to play the card game Bid Whist all the time.

They even had my older siblings learn how to play just in case they needed someone to fill in. My older siblings all enjoyed playing the game and still play it today. My younger brother and I never learned how to play the game, and frankly, it never appealed to me. Every so often, my brothers and sisters would play and asked me if I wanted to learn how to play, but I never got into gambling or card playing. However, the drinking and smoking I watched my parents engage in with their friends appealed to me more than learning to play Bid Whist, and it left a major impact on my life. Most likely, if a household has adult drinkers and smokers, the children will follow that same pattern. My parents' wild weekend parties with drinking and card playing set an example that I would mimic for many years to come. My siblings were divided when it came to drinkers and smokers. Four of us didn't drink or smoke, and four of us did.

As I adjusted to my new neighborhood, I eventually met the girl next door who was the same age as me. We started hanging out at the playground with a couple of other neighborhood girls about our age. One day, it started raining, and the four of us gathered under one big umbrella. One of the girls pulled out a cigarette, lit it up, and asked the rest of us if we wanted a puff. I didn't even hesitate to accept the cigarette. Watching my parents smoke, and being excited that the neighborhood girls included me, made me eager to give it a try. While choking and coughing after that first puff, feeling as though my heart was going to fall out of my chest, I wondered if it was even worth it. Unfortunately, smoking became a habit that I couldn't break for the next twenty-five years.

For some reason, I was hooked after that first puff, but I was only ten years old so I couldn't go out and buy my own cigarettes. Luckily, or unfortunately, everywhere I went there were people smoking. My parents were both smokers and so were most of their friends. I would go around my house looking for cigarette butts in the ashtrays, and I used to love it when my parents had company over because I got to smoke cigarettes more often. I would steal leftover cigarettes then hide in a room or the basement somewhere puffing away. I'd gotten the hang of smoking and enjoyed doing it. My parents had no clue what I was doing. Kool Menthols was the brand my parents smoked, so, of course, I started out with Kools. My dad used to accuse my sister Wendy of taking his cigarettes and would beat her whenever he found the butts under the steps of our front porch. Of course I was the one who was taking his cigarettes, but I could never admit to it. He would have killed me if he found out that his 10-year-old "pumpkin," as he affectionately called me, was smoking. My sister still gets mad at me to this day if the subject comes up because I never stepped up and said it was me. She claims he wouldn't have punished me because he always spoiled me.

It's sad and unfortunate that children can do many things undetected by their parents. Many kids get involved in smoking, drugs, skipping school, dating, having sex, and watching porn all without their parents' knowing. This is unfortunate because it causes children to get caught up in certain behaviors and addictions that will become struggles for them later on in life.

When I was almost twelve, I was introduced to alcohol at my sister's wedding. My second-to-the-oldest sister, Carol, got married and had a reception at my parents' house. While all the adults were drinking and having fun, my cousin Kristy (the sister of my new brother-in-law), Anita, and I went around with our empty glasses collecting wine and beer or whatever other forms of alcohol was left in guests' glasses and poured them into our own glasses. Before we knew it, we all had full glasses of alcohol. We also collected cigarette butts, and then we found an empty room upstairs away from the crowd and drank and smoked together like we were grown. That was the first time I combined cigarettes and alcohol, and it was an awesome experience!

The summer before junior high school, I got my first summer job working at a recreation center at the school across the street from my house. I helped manage the games and equipment for the center. I opened my first bank account with my first paycheck at age thirteen. It was an awesome feeling to have my own money, especially since I didn't have to do anything demeaning for it like when I was eight years old. Except for the fifty-dollars I was required to save, my father let me decide how I wanted to spend my money every time I got a paycheck. I bought school clothes with what I was allowed to keep.

My first crush was on a guy I worked with named Tayon. He was really cute. He acted like he was into me the entire summer while we were working together. One day, somebody brought in some weed, and we walked down the street on our lunch break and smoked it. When we returned, we couldn't stop laughing! We laughed for the rest of the day, but nobody noticed how silly we were acting or the fact that we were high. By thirteen, I had experienced sexual abuse and been introduced to cigarettes, alcohol, and marijuana. What were the odds that I would make good choices as I moved further into my teenage years? I might've had more productive habits if my life hadn't changed again so drastically a few weeks after I started junior high.

When I was twelve, my mother left my father for good. Although it didn't affect me initially, as I look back on the day my mother left, I realize that her leaving had a major impact on the way the rest of my teenage years played out. When my mother left, she went to stay with my older sister and her family. She was supposed to just stay there until she found somewhere to live, then she would come back for the three of us she left at home. My mother had left home a few times before, but eventually came back home willingly or my father would locate her and forcefully bring her home if she was gone longer than a couple days to a week. She would sometimes go stay with my sister or at times go to South Carolina where her family lived. I used to wonder how she got to South Carolina, but I later found out that my older siblings used to help get her there. For as long as I could remember, my mother would often say that as soon as my brother Anthony turned ten, she would leave my father. I just didn't know that it meant leaving me and my other two siblings as well.

I remember coming home from school one day and not finding my mother there after work. She had just gotten a job working at Bethesda Naval Hospital in Bethesda, Maryland, and she would normally be home when I got home from school. That day, I got home later than usual because I was on the school track team and had to attend practice.

I asked my baby brother, "Where is momma?"

He said, "She's gone and not coming back."

"She left?"

"Yea, she left daddy."

I felt relieved and so did my other siblings as the good news of my mother finally leaving my dad spread to each of us. We used to try to coerce my mother into leaving my father after every beating, and either she wouldn't leave or she would leave briefly and return.

One day after my mother moved out, I caught the bus after school to go visit her at my sister's house, but she wasn't home from work yet. At that time, she had changed jobs and was working in downtown D.C. at a little hot dog shop on Connecticut Avenue. (They sold the best sauerkraut.) As I was waiting for my mother to come home, I saw my father's car pull up with my mother in it. I went outside to greet her, but she was crying. My father had gone to her job, waited for her to get off, grabbed her from the bus stop, and forced her in his car; he then took her to a spot and raped her before bringing her to my sister's place. My mother's leaving had turned my father into a monster.

With the chaos and dysfunction that brewed at home, I needed an escape and some attention. I didn't get any attention from my father because he was too consumed with my mother and trying to drink his problems away. I didn't get the attention I needed from my mother because she failed to take me away from my father after she got consumed by her newfound freedom and her new relationship. So, after I started junior high school, I started to hang out with two girls who I really shouldn't have been hanging with. They weren't good influences at all, but at the time, their friendship was a welcomed relief from the chaos at home.

I was really glad to have the acceptance of those girls. Although I should have, I didn't really think about the things they wanted me to go along with. The fact that I chose these girls as friends was an early sign that I was moving towards the same dysfunction my parents exhibited. I remember one day when we didn't have money for lunch, and we decided to play hooky from school to go rob somebody. I don't know why I went along with such an aggressive approach to getting money, but at this point, acceptance was what I needed to cope with my home life. As we left school and walked through the area, we found this little old white lady down on Belmont Street carrying her purse on her wrist. We ran up to her intending to snatch her purse and keep running. However, this little old lady was stronger than we expected, and she wouldn't let that purse go even after we tugged at it for a few minutes. She eventually started to scream, so we had to run from the scene without the purse. Agreeing to engage in this type of activity showed that I was crying out for the attention and acceptance that I wasn't getting at home. I should have realized what would have happened had I gotten caught not just by the police but also by my father.

If children aren't taught to not steal or commit other crimes, then they won't know that what they're doing is wrong. One time when I got caught stealing candy from a local store, my father made me take the candy back, and he beat me right there in the store in front of everyone. The next time I was accused of stealing, I was actually innocent. My sister Syl had taken my sister Wendy and me shopping for Easter clothes at McBrides in downtown D.C. Wendy decided she wanted to take some earrings and some other stuff from the store and put them in her bag. The security guard caught her, and since I was with her at the time, I got grabbed also. They took us to a room and asked who we were with. When we told them we were with our older sister, they went to get Syl. They told her what we did and that we were going to jail for eighteen months for stealing. My sister begged and pleaded for them not to arrest us because we were just kids. They finally let us go after my sister said that she would take responsibility for us and tell our parents. I had no idea that Wendy was stealing, and I was innocent this time! Although I pleaded my innocence, we both got the beating of our lives. I'm sure Wendy was really happy that I got a beating for something I didn't do just like she did when she got blamed for stealing my father's cigarettes, which I actually stole.

Though I wasn't a fighter, I got into my first fight around that same time. The fight actually started over something silly. Someone told this girl Charlene that I called her a "redbone." I probably did. There was a group of cheerleaders in my school who were all redbones, and they paraded around school thinking they were all that and better than everyone else. Maybe it was jealousy, but I was annoyed by them. Charlene confronted me about it, and we started arguing. A crowd soon formed around us, and the crowd escalated the situation by chanting, "Fight!" repeatedly. The crowd really wanted to see a fight, so they got louder and louder. Neither of us gave in to the crowd's demands, afraid we'd get into trouble if we fought on school grounds. Then, someone suggested we meet outside after school. I didn't want to fight anybody, so I didn't really accept the suggestion.

When school was over, I tried to leave the building quickly before Charlene came looking for me. Well, she and the crowd found me walking home. I guess I didn't get out of there fast enough. The spectators continued to instigate the argument, trying to get us to fight. Then the crowd finally pushed us up against one another, and we started fighting. I was whipping up on that chick! When we finished, she wasn't a redbone any longer; she was pink! I was so excited to have my first fight and win that I ran home to tell my father. I thought he would be okay with me defending myself. That man tore my butt up and said, "You are not sent to school to fight but to learn!" I tried to explain how it happened, but it didn't matter because he said, "You don't fight in school or on your way home from school either." And my siblings thought I didn't get any whippings. Please!

Months passed, and my mother still didn't come for us. We would ask her every week when she was sending for us because my father was really out of control, but she never gave us a solid answer. My brother, sister, and I finally came to the realization that our mother wasn't coming back for us, and we soon found out why. My mother had acquired a male companion. His sister lived in the same building as my mother and sister, and they met passing each other at the complex. Then we found out that my oldest sister let my mother's lover move in with them. It baffled me as to how my sister allowed my mother to move that grown man in with them, especially when her little sisters and baby brother needed rescuing from the terror of their father. The whole situation angered me and changed my whole attitude towards my mother. First of all, how could a grown man stay with a woman who was living with someone else? If he really cared for her, why didn't he at least set up a place for them away from my sister and her children? Worse yet, my mother was sharing a room with her two young grandsons. What mother and grandmother would want to expose underage boys to such an arrangement? Talk about a dysfunctional family situation!

When my father found out that my mother had a new man who'd moved in with them, he became even harder to live with. We literally went through hell at home because of that whole situation! My dad started coming home drunk more often and even angrier. He would get us up out of the bed at three and four o'clock in the morning, tell us to get dressed, and make us walk to the bus stop to go to our sister's house. We had to walk about thirty minutes to the bus stop. When we got there, we had to sit in the cold on the bus bench for about two hours before the buses started running. Then we were on the bus half asleep and would miss school because my mother lived on the other side of town, and my dad was sending us there to try to disrupt what she had going on. By the time we would get to my sister's house, school would be starting. We would often have to stay at my sister's place until someone could come up with bus fare for us to go back to my father's house. The three of us had to sleep on the couch in the living room at my sister's until we were allowed to go back home. It wasn't comfortable being bunched up sleeping all together, especially when we had our own room somewhere else. All of this took a toll on us physically, mentally, and emotionally because we had to endure this torment several times a week over the course of three years. That's what my home life looked like during my early teenage years, and it attributed to why I made the choices to engage in drinking, smoking, and sex at the times I did.

As my parents continued to deal with their problems, putting their kids in the middle, my world didn't get any better; it only got worse. Being shuffled back and forth from my dad's house to my sister's place didn't get easier, just more and more frustrating. I blamed my parents for years for turning my world and my life upside down. I believe my life could have turned out so very different if I didn't have to deal with them and their problems.

I was looking forward to high school, which was supposed to be the highlight of my teenage years. However, because my home life was so jacked up, I didn't have a lot of hope that it would be great. Walking past all the upperclassmen outside and in the hallways on the first day of school made me extremely nervous. I heard people say, "goofy looking" and "hunchback," as I passed by them. I already walked with my head down, and hearing classmates talk about me like that made me keep my head down even more. I was already angry and in distress by the mess that was my home life, so hearing such negativity towards me didn't help my self-esteem at all. Needless to say, the start of high school as a freshman was pure torture! After the initial shock of entering the treacherous halls of high school, I began to see people I knew from my junior high school, which gave me some relief. Though I was a very bright, intelligent student with a good head on my shoulders, I let my family issues distract me and interfere with my ability to focus on school. With no real parental guidance, I changed direction and began to make some very poor choices. I started to hang out with my old friends whose lives were just as messed up as mine was. With all that I was going through at home, I really needed some positive influences, but instead I chose negative ones.

The things that we're exposed to or we experience as children are beyond our control. Children innocently trust their parents to raise them properly so that they can grow up to be productive members of society. Unfortunately, if some parents didn't have a good upbringing, they can't provide the same for their children. Sadly, the activities that parents engage in around their children can directly impact and affect their children's lives later on as adults. For the most part, many children aspire to be like their parents or they want to engage in the same activities they've seen their parents doing. If a child sees their parents smoking and drinking, and it seems to be making them happy, then the child, too, is going to want to be happy in the same manner as they've seen their parents. This is especially true for children who have witnessed any type of domestic violence between their parents. Witnessing domestic violence between parents is quite traumatic. So, when children witness their parents having a good time with one another with the inclusion of smoking and drinking, children may be apt to want to partake in the things they see their parents doing that is making them happy.

A large part of our lives are shaped by our environment and the people in our lives. Parents are actually supposed to be the main sharpening tool in a child's life. However, when the parent is dysfunctional, the children will inevitably be dysfunctional as well. Unfortunately, children caught in the crossfire of a dysfunctional upbringing will have no sense of control when it comes to making the right or wrong decisions in their own lives. A lot of the decisions we tend to make are shaped by our environment and someone in our lives we deemed credible, which is usually an adult in our primary household like parents or guardians. Whether our choice to engage in illicit activities is influenced by home or society, it's something that we can overcome, and a cycle we can break. In order to have a positive impact on the communities in which we live and on the next generation, we have to be proactive in breaking cycles in our lives.

Oftentimes, dysfunction can pass down from generation to generation where children can find themselves entering into similar behavioral patterns or situations that their parents lived through. This generally happens unknowingly as children grow older, live their lives, and make their own decisions. However, somewhere in the deep crevices of their subconscious, many of their decisions or choices are influenced by their upbringing. When children make the wrong choices, those decisions are based on their primary situations and from watching the adults in their lives. So, who is to blame? Is it the parents' fault their child made a bad decision during a vulnerable time? Could the child be blamed for their bad decisions although they weren't taught how to make proper decisions? Can they be held responsible for the impact or effect their wrong choices would have on them in the long run, or even the fact that there are consequences for bad decisions? Do we really expect children to function in dysfunction?

Just as one good decision has the power to impact and change the course of your life, so does one bad decision. However, with the bad decisions we make, we don't get to choose the consequences we have to face as a result of our poor decision-making. We have to be committed to breaking the cycle of bad decisions and teach the benefit of good decisions, especially the decision of salvation for our lives.

Reflection

Did you grow up with both parents?

_____

Did you have enough love and attention from your parents?

_____

If not, how did it affect you growing up?

_____

_____

_____

If you didn't have both parents growing up, what, if any, effect did it have on you?

_____

_____

_____

What are some behaviors, bad habits, or activities you engaged in as a child, teen, or even in adulthood that you believe were a result of the environment you grew up in?

_____

_____

_____

_____

Do you still have those negative behaviors or bad habits, or do still you engage in those illicit activities?

_____

If no, how did you break free from them?

_____

_____

What are you doing to break the cycle for the next generation in your family?

_____

_____

_____

_____

_____

If yes, would you like to break free from those behaviors, habits, or activities?

_____

_____

_____

_____

_____

Declaration

Pray aloud this Prayer of Freedom

Heavenly father, I thank you for your word and the power of your word. I thank you that the scriptures say that the truth shall make me free, and who the son sets free is free indeed. Therefore, I pray that as I have come in contact with the truth of your word, freedom is mine. I am free in Jesus Christ because he is my Lord and Savior. Therefore, I will no longer be bound by my past, and I will not let the enemy hold me hostage in my thoughts because of my past. I decree and declare that I am free from bondage, strongholds, behaviors, bad habits, and past activities, and I will not let anything keep me from my freedom. I am forgiven, and I walk in the liberty of forgiveness that God has given me. The blood of Jesus has cleansed me of all unrighteousness, and I have received God's love, grace, and mercy so that I can live a life that is free of sin, guilt, and condemnation. I thank you Father that I am free, free indeed!

Breaking Free

Pray. Commit to praying to God daily and asking Him to help you break free. Be open to people God may send your way as help.

Read the bible. Find scriptures you can use to pray and meditate on to help you change the way you think about the behaviors, habits, or activities you engage in. Romans 12:2 (NKJV) says, "And do not be conformed to this world, but be transformed by the renewing of your mind..." Changing your mindset will be vitally important to breaking free.

Become a member of a spirit-filled local assembly. Join a ministry that will teach you the word of God and help you build your faith.

Listen to the Word of God. Listen to the Word of God regularly via CD's, YouTube, or Facebook. Find some strong teachers and ministries you can listen to.

Get a support system. Find someone you can be accountable to and who can walk this journey with you.

Get counseling (if needed). Find a counselor or therapist who can help you navigate through things you have gone through and help you in moving forward.

Once you break free, will you commit to breaking the cycle for the next generation in your family?

_____

_____

_____

3

Young and Reckless

"You're getting an abortion," my parents told me when they found out I was pregnant. *Abortion*? I thought to myself. I had absolutely no idea what that meant. I was just as shocked as my parents to know that I was pregnant. First of all, I knew absolutely nothing about sex, let alone the possibility of getting pregnant, and I surely knew nothing about using birth control to prevent a pregnancy. After all, I was only fifteen years old, and no one had talked to me about sex, not my parents nor my older siblings.

When my father got into his crazy rages, I'd escape them by going to my sister's house. During one of those escapes, I met this guy named Dickie. He was much older than me: 21 years old as a matter of fact. He'd just gotten out of jail and was living with his mother, Miss Flo, and his sister, Pam. They lived on the 2nd floor above my sister's apartment. The day Dickie approached me, he did so in a playful way. I was sitting out front of my sister's apartment, and he walked over to me and said, "Hey girl, what's up? How you doing?" He had no idea he was approaching an innocent girl who lacked guidance, had a jacked-up home life, and had no one to talk to about the problems she was enduring. I thought he was nice, and the fact that he told me upfront that he'd just got out of jail made me think he wasn't trying to play games with me. That day, we talked about why he went to jail and what it was like. He was very handsome, and I was blinded by his color (he was light-skinned, which was my type).

While I was staying at my sister's apartment, I really didn't have anything to do while my mother worked. Although we'd just met, and there was no way he could've possibly liked me so fast, Dickie asked me to be his girlfriend. My immaturity kicked in immediately, and not knowing what I was agreeing to, I took the bait and told him, "Yeah, I would go with you," That's what we used to say back in my days when you agreed to be boyfriend and girlfriend. I have no idea what made me decide I wanted to be the girlfriend of a jailbird who was 6 years older than me, but he was a cool, ordinary guy. Every time I went to my sister's apartment for a visit, I'd hang out with him. He would take me around his friends and show me off like I was someone special. I must admit that him doing that made me feel special. He would also come to visit me at my father's house. He'd travel all the way from the Northeast side of town to the Northwest side just to see me when my father was at work and my siblings weren't home.

My mother and people in her apartment building suspected that Dickie and I were spending time together. My mother, as well as his mother and sister, tried to warn me about hanging out with Dickie. They said he was a bad influence, but I didn't listen to them when I should have. The one time my mother actually gave me good, sound motherly advice, I didn't follow it. Why didn't I listen? In hindsight, it was probably because she had never been a voice of authority in my life up until that point. After only about two weeks of knowing Dickie, he persuaded me to be intimate with him. It was the first time I'd ever had sex, and we only did it that one time. I had given up my virginity to a guy I barely knew.

One day following the incident, my sister Syl came to visit my father. I remember the day so clearly. She was in the bathroom doing something in the mirror, and I had to use the bathroom. I was feeling sick to my stomach like I had to vomit, and I rushed into the bathroom, bent over the toilet, and vomited over and over. While I was on my knees vomiting, my father heard me from wherever he was in the house, came straight in the bathroom, and said loud and firm, "You are pregnant!" Syl ran out of the bathroom quickly. I got up off my knees and said, "No, I'm not. I just have a bad stomach ache." My father knew I was pregnant before I knew that it was possible. I guess he knew because he'd fathered seven children all with the same woman. And just like that, I'd forgotten I'd even had sex. It's crazy that you can forget you had sex with somebody. How did I forget? I guess you can tell it wasn't a memorable experience. Or I just blocked it out of my memory and didn't want to remember. Maybe that's why it only happened once.

My father asked me who I had been with. I told him who the father was and where he lived. My father called my mother and gave her a few choice words, blaming her for my pregnancy. I wanted to yell out to him, *Hello! Your 15-year-old daughter you both neglected got pregnant. You both are to blame!* My mother was too busy with her new freedom from my father and with her new man Henry to be worried about me, and my dad was too busy drinking, bowling, and seeing a new woman every night. After all hell broke loose, my parents went back and forth about my pregnancy and what they were going to do about it. On her end, my mother went to see Miss Flo, Dickie's mother, expecting her to do something about it, but his mother said that was Dickie's problem, not hers. I still couldn't believe I was pregnant. I just knew my life was over. My parents decided that I wouldn't have the baby and would get an abortion.

The day was sunny and hot outside. My mother went to work without hugging me or even telling me anything consoling that I could've clinged to while I went to have the procedure. My father had paid for the abortion and designated my sister Annie to take me to get it. She called a cab and it drove us to an unknown place. We went inside and she signed me in with the receptionist. The lady at the front desk told her to come back at a certain time, then my sister left. There I was, fifteen years old and all alone without a clue about what was about to happen to me. I didn't know what to expect or what to do, so I just sat there waiting to hear my name called. The procedure was the most horrible experience ever and one that I never wanted to experience again! Afterwards, I was surprised to see my father was the one who came to pick me up. At that moment, I needed a mother or woman to help me through all I had just gone through! However, my father was nice, gentle, and compassionate towards me, and at that moment, I felt like his pumpkin again.

Dickie ended up going back to jail and had no idea what had happened to me. After all that I went through with the Dickie situation, I still didn't learn anything and put my vulnerable self out there again. Not long after the Dickie situation, I was sitting outside of my sister's apartment building when this guy named Leroy came over to talk to me. Leroy was the nephew of Miss Betty, who lived in the same building as my sister Annie and was one of her best friends. Leroy also had female cousins who I knew, but they were much younger than I was. Before long, Leroy and I became friends and then became a couple for about a month.

He was known as a decent guy with a good head on his shoulders. His older female cousins knew we had something going on, but none of the adults had any idea. I was enjoying the attention I was getting from these older guys; it fed my loneliness and low self-esteem. Leroy lived in Clay Terrace apartments in Southeast D.C. with his mother, and I would sneak off to his house every chance I got. She worked a lot, so he had the run of the house most of the time. He was eighteen, and I had just turned sixteen. We also had sex one time, which I truly didn't like. Afterward, I avoided him. He continued to pursue me on many occasions, but I never gave him the time of day again.

My interaction with boys didn't start with Dickie. It all started in 1974 when I was fourteen; I had my first "puppy love" crush on a guy named Fred. He was someone I really liked, and he really liked me. He was my best friend's brother. We'd flirted with each other over the years, but we never had a sexual encounter until we ran into each other years later when we were adults. When we were together growing up, he gave me a lot of attention and that made me miss him when we were no longer together. His sisters kept me informed of his whereabouts and who he dated. They told me he had gotten married once he joined the military and was stationed in North Carolina. I was heartbroken to know that he was married even though I was seeing someone at the time. His family and I were close, and his mother loved me as one of her own because she knew about my struggle with my parents. When Fred and I were seeing each other, his family thought for sure I was going to be his wife. I thought so as well. Like I said, it was puppy love. After we stopped seeing each other, the heartbreak lingered for some time, but his family and I remained close even after Fred had chosen to be with another woman.

When I was nineteen, Fred and I ran into each other during one of his visits home. Following that encounter, we kept in touch and would get together weekly, monthly, or anytime it was convenient to see one another. During our times together, we would talk about our younger days, his career, and at times, his wife. We even discussed how we both wished we were together. The reality of his marriage loomed over our relationship, but it didn't matter because we still decided to have an affair. His family knew of our sneaking around and didn't mind it because they didn't care for his wife. However, we didn't see each other much because he lived out of town and couldn't get away as often as he wanted. Eventually, we agreed to end the relationship because of my guilt and shame and his moving back into the area; we no longer wanted to risk getting caught.

Sleeping with a married man was one thing I truly had to ask God to forgive me for. Know that this truth was very difficult for me to share. So, as you are reading this part of my story, and if you've ever considered having an affair with a married person, I strongly encourage you not to do it! It will only hurt you, the intruder. Trust me, I know. Affairs cause deep emotional pain that takes a lot of time to overcome. Now that I am happily married and counsel women on this subject, I strongly advise them against intruding in someone else's marriage. This is one situation in my life that I didn't want to write about because it was hard to look back and face the immoral things I did in my dark days. Warning! Warning! Don't Do It!

By the fall of 1975, I'd already had two sexual encounters with two guys by the time I was 16 years old. What was I searching for, and what did I need from them? When I entered tenth grade at Cardozo High School, I met and began dating one of the football jocks. *Eric* was a well-known guy who was cool with everyone. He was behind two grades but was very handsome. I really can't remember how we met, but what I do know is we hit it off right away. I didn't think I was attractive enough for such a popular guy to approach me. To me, there was nothing special or significant about me that would make a guy choose me over the more popular girls. I wasn't the best dresser, my hair was normal (I'd never been to a hair salon at that time in my life), and I was tall and lanky. I was, as some would say, straight up and down because I had skinny legs, no boobs, and no butt. I wondered what attracted him to me, but I never asked. I was just taken by surprise that someone like him saw something in me that I didn't see in myself, or so I thought. He was very kind, nice, and treated me with respect.

When we started going together, it was the normal cute little stuff like talking on the phone a lot and smiling at each other when we saw each other in the hallway at school. As we moved forward into our relationship, I found out he was seeing another girl at the same time as me. It turned out that the girl and I had become good friends not even knowing we were dating the same guy. How clever was he? Even though we often talked to one another about our boyfriends, we never suspected we had the same boyfriend. One day, a mutual friend of ours came to me and told me that Peggy, my new friend, and I were both dating the same guy. I just knew that couldn't have been possible even though our boyfriends were both on the football team. I knew him by *Eric*, his first name, but Peggy knew him by his nickname, Kooda. Neither of us ever mentioned his last name, *Lawson*. Come to find out, that was the last name he used at school, but it wasn't his actual last name. As I investigated further, I found out that *Eric* and Peggy had been going together since junior high school. None of that bothered me though because *Eric* and I had hit it off and were doing our thing, and I felt he genuinely cared about me.

At that point, I began to play little games with Peggy. Although I really liked her, unfortunately, someone had to go, and it wasn't going to be me. I started asking her questions about her boyfriend. What was his real name? What position did he play on the team? Where did she meet him? She happily answered each question, which I already knew the answers to. As she told me more and more about him, I told her that it was strange that our two boyfriends were playing the same sport and even playing the same position. Finally, I asked her what her boyfriend's last name was. When she said his full name, I told her, "All this time, we have been talking about the same guy to each other." I told her he had given us different names to call him in school so we wouldn't find out about each other.

She didn't take the surprise too well, and to tell you the truth, I wouldn't have taken it well either. In fact, she left school crying right after our conversation. The next day, she brought her mother to school to talk to me about the situation. I didn't know what that was supposed to accomplish. It surely didn't change my mind about being with *Eric* because I was in too deep. When I told *Eric* that Peggy and I had both found out he'd been dating the both of us, he told me I was the one he really loved and stopped dating her. Peggy was beautiful with long black silky hair. She was loved by everyone who knew her from her neighborhood and where *Eric* hung out at the Boys & Girls Club in her area. I was a plain Jane compared to her, but it didn't matter because he chose me instead of her.

I was labeled the bad guy by a lot of the girls in my high school. Both upper- and lowerclassmen accused me of breaking up the longtime sweethearts. The girls from *Eric's* neighborhood gave me the hardest time when they found out what happened. Everywhere I turned, I heard whispers saying little stuff like, "Yeah that's her; I should punch her." I would go into the bathroom and hear another clique of girls whispering about me. It was awful! I guess everyone thought that *Eric* and Peggy would last throughout high school and college and eventually get married. Still, I was the chosen girl.

After our relationship was fully established with Peggy out of the way, I would hang out in the bleachers watching him at football practice, and he would sometimes walk me home after his practice. He would walk me to the corner of my street and then walk toward his house. My father had no idea that I was dating him, and I didn't want to get caught with him since the abortion situation wasn't that long ago.

At sixteen, I felt like I was old enough to make my own decisions, and dating was one of the things I felt I had a right to do. Besides, my parents were still tripping off their separation and consumed with their own new lives. As my jacked-up teenage years continued, going back and forth between my dad's house and my sister's place didn't get any easier, just more and more frustrating. Due to the instability, I had to give up the sport that I loved, and I lost close friends because I wasn't around. As a result, I started to focus more on boys rather than sports as an outlet for my frustration. I was good at sports, and I believe I could've been something greater with basketball in high school, college, or even could have gone on to play in the WNBA; that's how good I thought I was based on my sports accomplishments.

Who knows what could've happened if I didn't have to deal with all those dysfunctional issues at such a pivotal point in my life. I believe that after a while, they stopped caring about what I was doing or whom I was doing it with until I brought my new guy home one Thursday evening. My father was barely home, especially on Thursdays because it was his bowling night from 6:30pm until 10:30pm, and he didn't get home until around 11-11:30pm. But that night, lo and behold, my father left something, came back home for it, and found me and *Eric* chilling in the living room. When I introduced *Eric* to my father, he asked me how old Eric was. When I said he was eighteen, my father flat out said *Eric* was too old for me to date. I tried to tell my father that we were in the same grade, but he didn't care; he just knew that *Eric* was too old to date his sixteen-year-old daughter. I didn't think he cared what I did, but I guess I was wrong. My father ended the discussion by telling me I couldn't see *Eric* anymore. I had already disappointed him the year before, and I'm sure he didn't want it to happen again. Perhaps he knew I was still sexually active and didn't want me to end up pregnant again, or maybe he really cared. Although it had been a few years, I was still angry at the way things had been going since my mother left home. I decided right then and there that my father had no right to tell me who I could or couldn't date. So, I would sneak to go see *Eric* anyway. He lived about a ten-minute walk from my house.

We continued to date in spite of my father and the treatment I was receiving at school. Nothing mattered to me except my relationship with *Eric*. This was the first time I had actually been with a guy that long, and he was into me like no other guy had been except for the obvious reason—sex. I was *Eric*'s girl no matter what my parents thought or said. Besides, I was miserable at home with my father and from going back and forth to my sister's house. As delusional as it may sound, I enjoyed intentionally rebelling against my father. I felt like I deserved the right to treat him in such a way because of what he'd put me through during my childhood, especially after my mother left.

Eric and I would mostly meet somewhere and then go over to my sister's house or meet at his house. I started sneaking to his house every chance I got, which was mostly when my father would go bowling on Thursday evenings, and I would be back before he got home. We would sometimes chill at his house in the basement. *Eric* and his brother had the basement set up like it was a small apartment with a couch, chairs, a bed, lamps, a stereo, a television, and an old refrigerator for their food and drinks, including alcohol.

I became close to *Eric*'s mother during my visits, and she

really liked me. His mother didn't work, so she always saw who came and went in and out of her house. After a few visits of me hanging out on the porch and in the basement, she didn't have a problem with me staying in the basement as long and often as I did. *Eric*'s family became my escape because they didn't care that I was at their house all the time or how long I visited. They became my new family. Before I knew it, I was really falling in love with this handsome jock who paid a lot of attention to me.

When I became comfortable around *Eric*'s mom, he and I began to indulge in sexual behaviors during the week and on weekends at his mom's house but never at my dad's house. My mother didn't really care about us being together; she was too busy working and being in love. I'm not sure what happened to change my father's attitude toward me, but suddenly he started telling me to be home at a certain time and wouldn't let me do anything or go many places. He was constantly questioning where I was going and who I was with. Of course, I had to lie so he wouldn't know that I was still seeing *Eric*. My father even came to the school at the end of the day to check up on me. It got to a point that my friends started warning me if they saw him coming, and I would go hide somewhere in the building until he eventually left.

Even though I complained about how no one cared about me or what I was doing, when my father started exercising his parental authority again, his strict house rules became too much for me to bear. It was no longer about wanting my parents' love and attention; at that point, my freedom and my relationship was all that mattered. My younger brother Anthony and I were still at home waiting for a way to escape ever since my sister Wendy had left home after she told our father she was pregnant at the age of seventeen. My father wanted her to get rid of the baby, and she refused. She left to live with her baby's father and his mother.

That summer of 1976, I moved in with *Eric* and his family. I never understood why his mother allowed me to move in with them, but I was glad she didn't object to me living there. I found out as I was moving in that *Eric*'s brother's girlfriend was already living there; she was seventeen and pregnant. Before long, I became pregnant in March 1977. When I started back to school in the fall of my junior year, my pregnancy was barely showing, and I was almost six months pregnant. It eventually became impossible for me to stay in school while pregnant, especially since everyone knew I was carrying *Eric*'s baby. All the whispering about me was bad enough before I got pregnant, and when I started to show, it became even worse. Regretfully, I dropped out of high school in the middle of my junior year.

It's vitally important that mothers and fathers don't neglect their children, especially during the most formative years of their kids' lives. Parents must let their children know how special and beautiful they are and tell them that they are fearfully and wonderfully made according to God's Word in Psalm 139:14 (NIV): "I will praise you because I am fearfully and wonderfully made; your works are wonderful, I know that full well." Children need to know this very early in life so they don't find themselves clueless in the same predicaments I found myself in. Older siblings should also look out for their younger siblings whether they're in the home or not; children need the protection and guidance of their older siblings as well.

While the father is the protector and provider of the family, the mother is the nurturer. She is the one who gives the love, support, and guidance her children need. So when children grow up without one or the other, the children are sure to make some detrimental decisions that will alter the course of their lives. While girls need the strength of their father, there's something about a mother's love that really holds things together in a girl's life. If she's not getting love from her father to make up for the lack of love from her mother, it is inevitable that she will begin consciously or subconsciously searching for love in all the wrong places and people. When she finds what or who she's looking for, a longing for love she's been lacking in the home, it will be difficult for her to let it go. A woman becomes loyal to her first love, even at the expense of hurting others or even herself.

Although the first seven years are the most formative years of our lives, our teenage years are the ones that shape our future because the decisions we make during that time will have the most impact on our adult lives. If we decide to drop out of school, it affects our ability to get a job and become a productive member of society. If we decide to have sex, we face the consequence of having a baby out of wedlock, contracting a life-altering disease, or even having an abortion that has a long-lasting impact mentally and emotionally. Using drugs or alcohol can also have long-term effects or even end in death.

Entering my teenage years without a stable family unit affected my life in many ways. I initially didn't recognize that I didn't really receive love from my father, and I didn't truly understand how much I needed my mother's love until she took it away from me when she left home and distributed her love elsewhere. This affected me deeply. With no real supervision from my father and no mother to teach me the ways of life, especially about womanhood and boys, I began to experiment with life through various ways at different times in my life.

Regardless of the life you had growing up, you can decide whether to be a victim or a victor. You become a victim by making bad decisions that will lead you on the path of destruction. You become a victor by making the decision to do better than the environment in which you were raised, to make good grades in school, to get a good job or career, to become a productive member of society, and to help others who are in or may have grown up in unfavorable home environments.

Reflection

Do you feel as if you grew up in a loving and nurturing household?

_____

_____

Do you think your life would have turned out differently or you would have made different decisions if you had both parents growing up?

_____

_____

_____

What are some things you wish your parents would have done differently in raising you?

_____

_____

_____

_____

If you are a parent, did you adapt some of the ways your parents raised you in how you raised your children?

_____

_____

_____

Are there some things that you wish you could have changed in the way you raised your children (if they are now teenagers or adults) which you believe that has played a part in some of the decisions they've made or some of the behaviors, bad habits, or actions they are or were involved in?

_____

_____

_____

_____

_____

_____

_____

_____

_____

Declaration

I am loved by God regardless of what has happened to me or what I have done. God is with me, and I am never alone. I can get through anything that may come against me. I am an overcomer, and the light of my life shines brightly so all may see.

As an overcomer:

Be bold and confident in knowing who you are in Christ. Your boldness and confidence in who you are in Christ will draw others to you and ultimately to Christ. You can use your story to help others heal from past trauma and hurt so that they can move forward in God's plan for their lives.

Be positive and don't allow negativity around you. Staying positive causes you to have a positive impact on others around you. Not allowing negative people around you helps you to stay in a good, positive place. Allowing negativity around you will pull you down and back in a low place. Stay positive and surround yourself with positive people so that you can continue to feel good about yourself, your situation, and propel you to a new place.

4

Surviving in Chaos

My world had crashed down around me when I discovered that my man, the father of my son, was "stepping out" on me. *Eric* had become a big drug dealer and a major player in our community. Living with him was blissful at first, but our relationship eventually sent me into a state of depression. I was stuck and miserable, and I didn't know how to get out. I thought that was the life I wanted, to live with the man I loved and raise our son together. Boy was I wrong. When the ecstasy of the relationship wore off and reality set in, I wanted out.

As a seventeen-year-old high school dropout living with my man who was a boss on the street, I thought I was living my best life and doing good. But after a while, I no longer wanted the life of sex, drugs, and alcohol. I was starting to suffocate living in the house with *Eric* and our son, his mother, and his brother, his brother's girlfriend, and their child. And I especially had grown tired of the traffic coming and going through the house where my young son lived. I was tired of my boyfriend's mother thinking that her son could do no wrong, which was crazy since she knew he was selling drugs. I had even gotten tired of getting high on drugs. I was especially tired of the meaningless sex after I found out that the relationship was a lie because I wasn't the only one he was having sex with. I was just tired!

My whole mindset changed when I realized that my dude was stepping out on me. It took me to a place where I knew in my heart that I didn't deserve to be. Although this man didn't physically abuse me, the way my father had abused my mother, I was being abused emotionally. I had become an emotional wreck knowing that I wasn't being treated like a woman who loved and respected her man should be treated. I thought about all the things that I had allowed boys and men to do to me over the years, and I was determined from then on that I would make men respect me. No longer would I let anyone treat me with anything other than the utmost respect that I desired and deserved. I kept telling myself that there are more fish in the sea, and there's a man out there who will love me and treat me with respect. But was I respecting myself enough to make such a demand?

After I got pregnant, *Eric* started selling drugs to make some extra money. His sister had been dating one of the heavy hitters in the drug game at that time, and he put *Eric* on in the game to get him started. I had my son James on December 31, 1977. He was a beautiful baby with coal black wavy hair. Excited to see me and meet their new grandson, my mother and father rushed to the hospital, and they tried to convince me to come live with one of them at their houses when we were released. I refused to go live with my father again.

The feelings I had towards my father and the choice I made to leave home were a direct result of the troubled home life he subjected me to. For years I blamed my father for my mother leaving, which was the primary reason for the path my life took. So when I had to decide where I would go after my son and I were discharged, I chose to go stay with my sister Annie and my mother for three months. They persuaded me that I needed the help, and they promised to look after my son when he woke up in the middle of the night.

My mother and sister absolutely kept their word and took good care of my newborn baby. They fed and bathed him everyday, and I didn't have to do anything. They did it all. While we were living there, my mother's boyfriend nicknamed my son Bootsy because he was born the night his father went to a Bootsy Collins show. *Eric* came by daily to visit us, and before long, I was back living in the house with him and his family. My dad still wanted me back home with him, and he harassed me constantly about it. After the way life had been in that household growing up, I couldn't imagine trying to raise my son around him. Not once did I consider that maybe having a grandchild around would've softened my father's once hard and angry nature. Besides, my *Eric* was actually taking good care of us with all the money he brought in from selling drugs. We never wanted for anything. I shopped and shopped all the time for things I couldn't imagine ever having the ability to buy. When I turned eighteen the next year, my father stopped harassing me about coming home.

After a couple of weeks of being back at *Eric's* house, I started taking my son back to my sister and mother so they could take care of him. They were all too happy about getting my baby boy back in their care. It got to the point that my mother wouldn't let me bathe, feed, or change him. Since my sister, mother, and my mom's boyfriend were taking good care of Bootsy, it gave *Eric* and me the opportunity to do whatever we wanted, go wherever we wanted, and return to pick up our son whenever we wanted. My sister did most of the caring for Bootsy because my mom worked, so *Eric* paid her a lot of money to keep our baby. Even though it was hard living with *Eric* sometimes, I still wanted to be in a relationship with him and to enjoy the "fab" life he was giving me. However, *Eric* eventually didn't care how long Bootsy and I stayed over at my sister's house. The streets were his world most of the time.

Later that fall, *Eric* went to college at Iowa State University on a football scholarship. He was twenty years old when he graduated from high school. I went to a few of his in-state games and even flew to Iowa to attend one of his games. Iowa was so cold that I vowed to never travel to that region ever again! *Eric* and I were still in love during his brief time away in college, and even though I was still his number one, the long distance relationship was very hard on me as a single parent. As it turned out, he didn't last long in Iowa and had to come back to D.C. I really thought it was because he wanted to be near his son and me, but he decided to come back and play football for a local college. I was very happy with his decision, at least at first. When he returned home, I soon discovered that something had changed, and he was different. He still treated me well, bought me anything I wanted, and provided for our son, but I could no longer go out with him and his friends anymore. Although he kept me in the latest styles, which I loved, he no longer allowed me to go anywhere with him except to the movies on some occasions. When I asked him why, he said he didn't want me around his boys and what they were doing. For a long time, I thought he was protecting me from the street life, and I never considered that there might be another female in his life.

Eric's football career didn't last much longer beyond that first year of college because he became too old to play college football. Everything changed once he stopped playing. His whole focus changed. He became one of the biggest drug dealers on our side of town. I was right there with him cutting, bagging, distributing, and smoking the drugs. The drug we sold back then was called Love Boat. It was known to make you get butt naked. The drug game was lucrative for the both of us, but it wasn't an easy life.

Even though Eric was very kind and nice to me, treated me with respect, and gave me just about anything I could possibly want, the nice things came with a heavy price. If I wanted to go shopping, I had to have sex with him even when I didn't want to. Anytime I wanted money to go somewhere with my family, I had to have sex with him. He wanted sex anytime during the day or night, and I had to oblige, especially if I wanted something. I was basically being treated more like a hoe or a prostitute versus a girlfriend or "baby mama." This cycle went on for a few years until I got bored and tired with the sex and the relationship. It had gotten to a point where I would think back to when I was eight and my uncle used to give me money to touch me. I had to give up something to get something that I wanted. It used to make me angry and bitter to think about the situation I was in and had to go along with all because I didn't want to live at home with my father. The sex became like a job, and I began to use more drugs than I sold just to get through the meaningless, lackluster routine.

I did some immoral things by using my body and selling drugs to get the best life for my son, even if I was doing them with and for my man. We lived comfortably for a few years until the relationship changed. I was going through depression and felt like I was stuck in a place that I couldn't come out of. Don't get me wrong. At times, the sex was on point and the relationship was too, but the good times wouldn't last long. We would argue a lot about the baby, him being away from the house all the time, why he didn't take me out anymore, and other crazy stuff. I was tired of being a make-believe wife washing and ironing his clothes, cleaning up behind him, and cooking his food. It was okay at times, but some days, I just wanted to scream at the top of my lungs for someone to get me out of that mess of a life I was in. The only thing I did to escape my life at those times was to go visit my family on weekends. *Eric* went with me most times, but eventually he stopped. My family liked him a lot because he took good care of me. I was always well-dressed, which made me become sort of a bougie type of gal.

One time I found out that *Eric* had given me chlamydia. I went to his mother, thinking since we were cool that I could talk to her about anything, especially since she had been there for me like a mother. But when I told her about the infection, she cursed me out so bad that I wanted to leave that house right then and there and never return, but I had no one else to turn to or anywhere to go, or at least anywhere that I wanted to go to. I learned my lesson that day: you can't ever talk about a momma's boy to his mother, especially when it's not anything good. I learned that a mother will always take her son's side even when she knows it's a possibility that her son is in the wrong.

When we were selling drugs, we made so much money that we never bothered to count it. *Eric* used to carry the money around in an attaché briefcase with combination locks on it, but he would never give me the combination. He said I didn't need to have it because he supplied what I needed. He didn't know what I needed. He thought he knew, which he said was money or clothes, but what I really needed was to break free from that relationship.

Here's a crazy story. So one day I met up with one of my best friends, and we went to visit my father and little brother. *Eric* had me keep the briefcase until he came to pick it up. Out of curiosity, I wanted to see if I could open the briefcase. I went to the kitchen and got a butter knife out of the drawer and found a pair of my dad's pliers. She and I tussled with the briefcase until we lifted up a corner of it just enough to slide the butter knife through back and forth until dollar bills were coming out and hanging onto the knife. We were so amazed that we did it, and we plotted to get as much money out as we could. Even though he never counted the money, we got nervous after we counted how much we had gotten out of the briefcase, which was almost five hundred dollars. We laughed and joked about it for a few minutes. When we finished counting, we split the money and continued visiting with my dad and brother. I knew it was wrong to steal, but in essence, I wasn't stealing because I helped get the money, and I worked for it just as he had. When *Eric* picked me up that evening, I was cool as a cucumber like nothing ever happened.

After a while, I grew tired of trading sex for things, and I decided to get a job because I wanted to be able to get what I wanted without having to have sex for it. I got a job at Georgetown Hospital working in the medical records department. Getting that job was the start of my independence and some necessary lifestyle changes to set me on a new path of life.

Foundation - the basis or groundwork of anything; the moral foundation of both society and religion. The home we grow up in and the way our parents raise us build our moral foundation and set the course of our lives. If we don't have a proper or solid foundation through discipline, guidance, morals, or values, our lives will be destined to go in the opposite direction of what God intended. But Grace be unto God for our lives were already predestined by Him for His glory (Ephesians 1:5-11); by his divine nature, He repairs the foundation laid in our lives so that we can get back on the path He ordained for us.

The foundation of my life was cracked before I really knew it, and this cracked foundation set the course for the bad choices I would make throughout my young adult years as different situations were presented to me. Unfortunately, my parents didn't adequately provide me with everything that I would need to successfully navigate into adulthood, let alone motherhood. My parents were poor examples as to what parenting and adulthood should look like.

When we don't have proper nurturing and love from our parents, we tend to think, "If I'm on my own, I'd be just fine." We think that being "grown" at a young age is "living the life." But it actually puts on us a burden that we don't have the strength to carry due to our immaturity. Eventually, we find ourselves at a point in our lives where we are weak and vulnerable, and we wish we were back in the care of our parents where we should've been all along. Luckily, our omniscient and omnipotent God will always orchestrate our path through situations and circumstances to not only get us back on the path we're supposed to be on, but He will also give us the adequate resources we need to help us navigate through life.

Reflection

Are there decisions that you made when you were younger that you feel are a direct result of your upbringing?

_____

_____

_____

Did you do things or make certain decisions because you were trying to get back at your parents?

_____

_____

_____

Have you forgiven your parents and yourself for your less than perfect past?

_____

_____

If not, there is no better time than now to forgive yourself and your parents to free yourself from the past.

Are there things that you are still holding on to from your past that could be affecting your present life?

_____

_____

_____

_____

_____

If so, make the decision right now to release those things and free yourself from the past. Jesus told us in John 8:36 (NKJV), "Therefore if the Son makes you free, you shall be free indeed."

Your freedom from the past is important to God. He does not condemn you for your past; He has forgiven you and desires that you live a full life.

Read the story of the Samaritan woman in John 4 and the story of the woman caught in adultery in John 8.

After reading these stories, can you now see yourself through the eyes of Jesus and not through the lens of your past?

_____

_____

_____

What are some things that you would like to do differently so that you may live a life of freedom and purpose?

_____

_____

_____

_____

_____

5

Face to Face

There comes a point in our lives when we have to come face to face with ourselves and ask, "Do you like what you see?" That face-to-face moment came for me at my mother's funeral. On March 21, 1981, my mother died of kidney cancer at the age of forty-six, just four months shy of my twenty-first birthday. One of my sisters, was a member of the church where the funeral was held. As I sat through my mother's funeral, I looked at my siblings and wondered how they seemed to have more solid, stable lives than I did. I was the one living the glamorous lifestyle with all the material things to show for it. I had just about everything I wanted, and I could get what I wanted when I wanted it. Money and things were no problem for me. However, how I looked on the outside with all the glitz and glam didn't match how I felt on the inside. Truth be told, I was depressed. I felt like I was stuck in a destructive cycle and really needed to get my act together. Not only for my sake, but also for my young son.

So, I guess my mother's funeral was the only way I was going to find my way into a church. It was not a place that was high on my agenda to go to seeing as though I hadn't been since I was a young child. I knew that I was tired of living the life I was living and wanted a change for me and my son, but never did I think that church would be the agent for my change. But there I was, back at the church the Sunday following my mother's funeral. As I sat through the service, I thought, *I might as well give this a try; this may be exactly what I need to get my life on a better path than the one I was on.*

As I sat through the funeral service, I dwelled on some of the events in my life. Even though I visited my mother often at my sister's house, I still felt that if she had been there consistently to help me make better choices, I wouldn't have been in the position I was in. I felt like my father should have protected me from a family member who repeatedly took advantage of my innocence, even though I didn't speak up for myself. He should've known, some way, somehow, that something wrong was happening in his house to one of his children. I've always blamed my parents for my life. It's true they did not give me a good foundation as a child because I didn't learn how to make good choices, have healthy, meaningful relationships, or rely on God when life threw me a curve ball. I never learned to take responsibility for my decisions or my actions; the problems in my life were always someone else's fault. But the time had come for me to face the truth that my life was a mess because of the choices I'd made. On top of that, I had a young son whose life was affected by those choices as well.

As I sat amongst grieving family and friends, I wondered if my sister's church could be the place where I could make a new life for myself and my child. I knew I needed to get Bootsy away from the drug culture and unstable relationship with his father; I wanted something better for him. Knowing I had to make some changes in my life and seeing that church as the opportunity to do so, I returned to church the following Sunday.

Although I honestly don't remember what the sermon was that day, I decided that joining that church was a good place to start with turning my life around. At the end of the service, I asked one of the members what I needed to do to join their church. I was given a packet of information and asked to fill out a membership card. Then I was invited to begin attending the New Members class. They had programs for my son to attend as well, so I decided this was what I was going to do. At that point, I had some other decisions to make, like where to live and how to earn a living for the two of us that didn't involve anyone from my "old" life.

I talked with my father after my mother's funeral. He'd changed. It appeared he'd made some life-altering choices as well. He invited my son and me to move in with him. When I told him I would like to do that, he seemed super happy at the possibility of having me back in his life again. The day I packed my belongings and walked away from that old life, it was as if this heavy burden was lifted off of my shoulders. I was filled with so much joy inside; I can't even begin to describe it. I was on a new path, and I knew things would finally change for the better for my son and me.

I was a young mother who had gotten used to having everything she needed for herself and her child, except stability. Though I was excited about the path I was on, I really didn't know what to expect from this new life, these new people, or my father. They all seemed very friendly and caring, but I was a severely wounded, young woman who needed an environment that would keep me and my child safe. So, would returning back to the place where I was wounded help me on my path to a new life? I didn't know for sure, but I decided to give it a try, especially after seeing the difference in my father. I sincerely hoped this would be a way to protect my child and help me begin to make better decisions that would bring about the change I knew in my heart had to happen. My mother's death had brought me to a crossroad in my life, and God used her funeral to draw me away from the old life and into a new one.

So I faithfully attended church and sat through the New Members class for four weeks. There was an official graduation ceremony at the end of the four weeks, and at that ceremony, I was extended the Right Hand of Fellowship on April 26, 1981. The woman who taught the New Members class told us that after we finished her class, we weren't to just sit in the pews every Sunday; we were expected to become an active part of the church's ministry. She also advised us to think about the gifts God had given us as a way of deciding which ministry to join. I had no idea what that meant, but I agreed with the pastor when he said the young people's choir was the best choir on this side of heaven. I had always wanted to sing, so I decided to join the choir.

My first visit to choir rehearsal was awkward and strange. As I entered the room, the tenor and alto sections were shouting out, "She can sit over here in this row." Thinking that was a good place to start, I went to sit with the altos and tried to blend in with them. It didn't take long for them to decide that was not a good match for my voice. I was moved to the tenor section, which was a much better match for my heavy voice. The choir had a really great sound, and I loved how they sang in parts to produce that "heavenly harmony."

Though I was excited about joining the church and the choir, I was still leery of allowing anyone to get too close to me for fear they would find out I came from "the streets." I had lived in a world of sex, drugs, and alcohol, and I was an unwed mother. As far as I knew, none of these people had any knowledge of me or where I came from even though my sister was a member there. My thinking was since these people were already members of this church and were actively involved, then they were free from the worldly life, and I hoped they could help me really begin to change. Boy was I wrong! Even in church, you can't judge a tree by where it's planted but only by the fruit that it bears.

As time went on, I began to make friends with the members. Two of my new friends were Terri and Tammy. We are still friends today. One day, they told me that when I came to choir rehearsal that first day, everyone believed I was acting like I thought I was better than others. I'm not sure what gave them that impression, unless it was the way I was dressed. It's really sad how people judge you or formulate an opinion about you based on your outer appearance without even saying one word to you. After Terri and I became sisters in the Lord, she told me that along with a few others, she didn't like me at first. The truth is, I was nervous about how I was going to fit into this new environment and perhaps overcompensated by appearing too confident. I was dealing with a lot of emotional wounds and had my protective shield up.

When I joined the church, I truly felt that I was led there by the Lord even though my first visit there was for my mother's funeral. Something was pulling me in and stirring within. I had no idea what God had in mind for me, but I knew deep within that this was the beginning of the change I needed to get my life right before it was too late. Since I was almost twenty-one and had a child, I thought it was appropriate to hang around older people. I think I was looking for a new family who would give me guidance as to how to walk in this new life. In search of maternal guidance, I hung out with a woman who I now affectionately call my Aunt Sandra, as well as with Terri's mother, Peaches. And there was also Deaconess Pearl Allen, well until she later found out that I was dating her son Jonathan.

After choir rehearsals, everyone usually gathered to talk before leaving. One day I encountered this tall, dark, handsome guy who I believed had his eyes on me as well. We said a few things to each other mixed with a few flirtatious comments, which sparked something in me. Following our first encounter, we would exchange flirty remarks at rehearsals and performances. In May 1981, I attended Aunt Donna's baby shower, which turned out to be one of the best days of my life. On that day, my angel Jonathan Allen and I connected on another level. We talked to each other all day. He told me he was eighteen, which meant that he would have been turning nineteen on his birthday that August. I was twenty going on twenty-one that July, so I didn't see any harm in talking and flirting with him even though I was a little older. However, I found out later, after we became close, that he was really sixteen years old. What a bummer...This boy was still a kid!

Members of the choir began to suspect that Jonathan and I were seeing each other. When Jonathan's parents, Deacon Joseph and Deaconess Pearl Allen, found out I was the older woman "corrupting their baby boy," as they put it, all hell broke loose. It reminded me of high school when I was dating *Eric*, and it turned out everyone blamed me for his breakup with his former girlfriend. Now, though, it was perceived that I was an older woman with a baby out of wedlock who was looking for a father for her child as well as stealing the most eligible bachelor in the church from the young ladies who had been groomed to be his future wife. From what I heard, all the young girls in the church were vying to marry the young Minister Jonathan Allen, but then I came along. Mothers and their daughters hated me, and I had to deal with gossip and being the outcast all over again.

Despite the opposition from his parents and the leaders of the church, Jonathan and I continued to be together. We both knew that we were meant to be together. Jonathan was scheduled to preach his initial sermon in September 1984, but the church found out through one of my so-called friends that

I was pregnant, and the sermon was cancelled. The church wanted me to follow their "sinners protocol" and go before the Deacon board to confess what we had done. If I confessed, then Jonathan could preach. I was so upset that I told them, "No, I am not going to do what you are asking with as much dirt going on in this church." At that point, I no longer liked being a member there because they were hypocrites. Most of the young folks were doing worse things than we were, yet we were the ones being singled out and stoned. I guess that's what happens when your secret sins have visible consequences.

In spite of the gossip and ridicule we received within the church, we continued to attend the services, and we finally married on November 21, 1984. Jonathan preached his initial sermon on March 8, 1985. Some years later, Jonathan was eventually appointed the youth minister for the church, and I stayed there for the sake of my husband, miserable for years. I hoped that God would answer my husband's prayers to start our own church, and the Lord was faithful because Jonathan was later called to start a church. There was one issue at hand that I was not expecting: right after Jonathan gave his notice that we were leaving the church in September, the pastor asked Jonathan to stay until the end of the year. I was like, *I am not staying at this church another Sunday after what they wanted to put me through!* I decided to stay home from church from September to late December and let Jonathan bide his time there by himself. Jonathan started Gospel Missionary Baptist Church on December 31, 1996, in the basement of our home in Fort Washington, MD. We had approximately fifteen to twenty people join us that night.

Jonathan and I moved forward with our new lives and new ministry. It would have been great to have my mother-in-law to look up to as a mother and a wife since my mother was deceased. Unfortunately, that didn't happen because I was the older woman who stole her sixteen-year-old son, who was her baby boy when we first started dating. Back then, I didn't care about the age difference, but I sure can relate to it now that I am a mother. Deaconess Pearl Allen and I became cordial to one another after Jonathan and I got married, but we didn't get close until many years later although I was close to the rest of the Allen family. His father and grandmother accepted me and made me feel welcomed into the family. I guess they figured the damage was already done and to just go with the flow. Not long after Jonathan and I were married, his other two brothers got married too. Although all three sons were married, only two of the daughters-in-law were allowed to call my mother-in-law mom, and that didn't include me. She never invited me to call her mom, and that really hurt. The three of them would go shopping together and even went on a trip together, but I wasn't invited. I felt so rejected and treated like an outcast, so I avoided his family. When I did go around them, it was only because Jonathan asked me to. Since there were a few family members who did like me, I still had a good time when I did attend their family events.

Tired of the distance between my mother-in-law and me, I wrote her a five page letter expressing how it hurt me to not be allowed to call her mom like the other two daughters-in-law. In the letter, I asked her why we couldn't have a relationship and why she didn't come to her only grandchild's first birthday party. After she read the letter, she came to me, and we had a long conversation about our relationship, or the lack thereof. Afterward, I was allowed to start calling her mom. She even helped me get a job in the school where she worked. I started working as a teacher's aide in 1989 at Burrville Elementary in Northeast, D.C. where my youngest son attended, and I worked there for two years. I didn't even have my high school diploma at the time, and I was still able to get this kind of job not once, but twice, by the favor of God!

Following our heart-to-heart conversation, my mother-in-law and I became the best of friends until she died. I was very happy at our new friendship, and it filled a void and emptiness left by my own mother after she died. My mother-in-law became ill from an infection in her pacemaker. Although they changed the pacemaker, the infection didn't get any better. While she was on her sick bed, I was there for her daily, taking care of her as if I was her nurse. I was a stay at home mom at the time, so it wasn't an inconvenience for me to take care of my mother-in-law. I cared for her the same way I would have cared for my own mother had I known she was as sick as she was before she died. My mother-law-died in 1991, and her death was very painful for me as I had grown attached to her once our relationship evolved.

In 1988, I went to Calvinade Cosmetology School in Washington, D.C., for eleven months. One Thursday while Jonathan and I were driving, I saw a "Hiring" sign in the window of a salon on Florida Avenue in Northeast D.C. I went in to apply for a shampoo tech position. I told the owner that I had just graduated from cosmetology school, and I was a nail technician also. She said to me, "You are a stylist and nail tech, not a shampoo girl." She offered me a job, and I started that following Saturday. I worked as a nail technician a few days a week and a stylist a few days a week until my clientele picked up. The owner was very nice and trained me in a lot of areas to perfect my craft to be a great stylist. I was excited about this new venture and was eager to learn all that I could in multiple areas. She taught me better techniques on how to shampoo, apply chemicals, and color, and she also taught me how to do my clients' nails better. She also owned a boutique above the salon, so she showed me how to sell clothes to the customers too. She was also a product representative for Dudley's Hair Company, one of the most prestigious black hair care companies back then, and she trained me on working with their products. We would travel to different salons to train stylists on how to apply Dudley's products. I was doing so well working in the salon that I had my own key to open and close the shop.

Everything was going well until she decided to start sleeping with her product sales representative. This didn't sit well with me because she was married and a Christian. Every time we had to do a show out of town, the guy would show up. She and I shared a hotel room, and it got pretty gross for me anytime I was in one bed and they were in the other bed having sex right there with me in the room. I hated it with a passion. She lacked class and discretion, and it disgusted me all the more because it wasn't just me she did it in front of; she also did it in front of another stylist and her goddaughter who traveled with us sometimes. At first I felt like it wasn't any of my business because she was grown, and if that was what she wanted to do, who was I to tell her otherwise. It never dawned on me that as a Christian and a pastor's wife that I should've spoken to her about her behavior. Then it became my business when she started asking me to lie to her husband and kids about her whereabouts. Initially, I didn't tell my husband, but when he saw that I was unhappy with working at the salon, I had to tell him what had been going on. I told him I no longer wanted to go to the shop and wanted to quit. When he asked why, I filled him in on everything. After that, he started working on building me a shop upstairs in our house, and he asked me to hold on until he could get the shop completed. I held on as long as I could until one day I decided I couldn't take it any longer and quit.

The second school I worked at, Shadd Elementary, was in the worst neighborhood in the whole city as it was where all the drug dealers lived and hung out. I worked there from 1992-1995 in the pre-K department. One day as I was working as the playground monitor, a little girl who looked to be about five years old came up to me and said, "Hi, mommy." I looked around, wondering who she was talking to, but she looked at me and said it again. Later on when I was the cafeteria monitor, the same thing happened. She had told all the other children that I was her mommy. When I asked the kindergarten teacher who the girl was and why she was calling me mommy, she said, "If you saw her mother, you would see why she wants everyone to think you are her mommy!" I didn't know how to respond to that statement, but I definitely became curious to find out more about this little girl and her mother.

I made arrangements to meet her mother, who was actually her aunt who was raising her, and I discovered that she was on crack. She was probably about twenty-seven years old, but she looked like she was over fifty. After meeting the aunt, I asked her if the little girl could come and visit me for the weekend. She agreed and what happened next truly shocked me. She showed up at the school that Friday with a bag of dirty, faded clothes and said she could go home with me. From that moment on, I was determined to do what I could to help this little girl have a better life. She would come to school on Fridays with a bag of clothes and would spend the weekend with me; that became our routine for years. I started buying her nice clothes and took her to church with me. She eventually started coming to stay with us during the summer as well. Then I found out that she had two younger sisters in preschool. When I saw the sisters together, I realized that the two younger sisters looked to her as if she were their mother, and they did whatever she told them to do. She was practically raising her two younger sisters. So, I started helping with her sisters as well. Their dad was a drug addict as well who allowed others to come into their home to get high. The drug dealers in the neighborhood saw what I was doing for these little girls and protected me. After their drug dealer father was shot in front of them, their aunt, a functioning addict, was raising them alone, so I remained a constant mother figure to them.

I eventually left that school after several years. A rumor had circulated amongst the teachers that my husband, the pastor, was a drug dealer. The rumor started after my husband bought me a brand new BMW, and since I was picking up the little girls from the drug area, they thought it just had to be true. It was the worst thing ever for me to be accused of such treachery. The main teacher I worked with turned against me after we had been close for many years of working together. It was hard to experience, but I learned that someone who you call a friend can be jealous of you. I wanted to quit right then and there; I just couldn't take the backstabbing. My husband encouraged me to hold on long enough so that when I did quit, I wouldn't have to work again until I decided. He was making enough money that I could stay home. He believed that if his wife decided she didn't want to work, then it was his job to make it happen for her. After leaving that job, I haven't worked in the last twenty-five years.

Things had gotten so out of control with the rumors that one day I just quit on the spot. The drama was too much for me to handle. I found myself explaining to the other teachers that my husband had a very good job and was able to upgrade some areas of our life, and the car was just the beginning. It wasn't because he was dealing drugs or getting paid by the church. But they just wouldn't listen to me, and I couldn't take the jealousy anymore. As far as the girls, I still have a relationship with them to this day. When the oldest sister had her first child, she named her daughter Jakala, which is sort of an acronym for Jonathan And Kim Allen's Little Angel! All of her children call me grandma!

Forgiveness is something God commands of us. Not only are we required to forgive others, but it is essential that we forgive ourselves. If we don't forgive ourselves for the wrong we did or the bad decisions we've made, we will live our lives in guilt and condemnation, which will stop us from walking fully in our purpose. Romans 8:1 (KJV) states, "There is therefore now no condemnation to them which are in Christ, who walk not after the flesh, but after the Spirit." So if you have asked God for forgiveness, knowing that He has forgiven you, you can be free to forgive yourself as well as others.

Guilt and condemnation will keep us in bondage to our past. Jesus said in John 8:36 (KJV), "If the Son therefore shall make you free, ye shall be free indeed," and that gives us the right to be free from our past. When we're free, we stop putting the blame on others and accept responsibility for our actions. Freedom causes us to grow, develop, and mature in our decision-making abilities. If we make the wrong choices, we are mature enough to accept the responsibility and consequences for those decisions and not blame others. That is why it is essential to be filled with the Holy Spirit; He is the Spirit of Truth who helps us in our decision-making. When we follow the Holy Spirit, we make all the right, Godly decisions for our lives and any lives our decisions will impact.

Reflection

When did you finally come to a turning point where you finally had to take responsibility for your own life?

_____

_____

_____

Have you come face to face with yourself and realized that the path you are on is wrong, and it's time for a turnaround?

_____

_____

_____

_____

_____

If not, now is the time to face yourself and make that first step for change.

Are there some areas in your life where you would like to see a difference?

_____

_____

_____

What are those areas?

_____

_____

_____

_____

_____

As stated before, Romans 12:2 says be transformed by the renewing of your mind. So, what you will need to do is find scriptures that will help you to renew your mind about those areas you would like to change. When you find the scriptures, read them, study them, and meditate on them. Then listen to preaching and teaching messages on the areas you would like to see different in your life. For example, if you are having issues with cursing, gossiping, talking negatively, or complaining, here are few scriptures that you can use to help renew your mind and transform what comes out of your mouth.

Ephesians 4:29 (NLT) *Don't use foul or abusive language. Let everything you say be good and helpful, so that your words will be an encouragement to those who hear them.*

Philippians 2:14-15 (NLT) *Do everything without complaining and arguing, so that no one can criticize you. Live clean, innocent lives as children of God, shining like bright lights in a world full of crooked and perverse people.*

Colossians 4:6 (NKJV) *Let your speech always be with grace, seasoned with salt, that you may know how you ought to answer each one.*

6

Living in Two Worlds

The church is known as the safe haven for the broken, dying, hurting, and the lost. The place of rebirth. The place where the hurting and sick are healed and made whole. The place where the lost, hopeless, and destitute find hope and life again. When you join a church, you expect your life to turn in a different direction, to take a different path. You expect to take the path that will lead to a life filled with godliness and away from death and destruction. It is not just the church, but the teachings, wisdom, guidance, instructions, and discipleship that you're receiving that help lead you toward living as a new creation in Christ, where old things are passed away.

What if you enter the church expecting to leave your old way of living, and the exact opposite happens? As time goes on, you're hit with, "I have set before you life and death, blessing and cursing; therefore choose life" (Deuteronomy 30:19 NKJV), but you weren't spiritually strong enough to choose life yet. You were so used to the side of death because it had all the appealing attributes of the flesh even from the church perspective, and it looked like you could do both. According to Romans 8:7, the flesh is enmity against God. As born again Christians, we try to live according to our flesh while trying to serve God at the same time, and we're creating unnecessary spiritual warfare for ourselves. We're placing ourselves in battles that we're not equipped to fight, especially as new believers in Christ. Thanks be unto God who is rich in mercy and is with us even when we're not fully in Him because He is preserving our lives for His purpose and calling for us, which was foreordained before the foundation of the earth. When you are living life for yourself and doing what you want to do, you give no thought or consideration to your future or even your purpose in life, let alone how your choices will affect others. As I look back over my life, I can clearly see that I was repeating my parents' cycle but in a different way.

During the time when I met my angel Jonathan, I was dealing with a whole other side of the church. After I became friends with some of the choir members, who were straight and gay, they invited me to go out and drink with them. Imagine my initial shock when I found out that the church members went out drinking. But I quickly dismissed it, and decided it must be okay if they were doing it while going to church and singing in the choir at that. We went to gay clubs the most because that's where we had the best fun. A lot of people thought that Terri, Tammy, and I were gay because we hung out with the gay people so much. They were our closest friends, and we went everywhere together. If you saw one of use, you saw the others. During our times out, we used to get drunk. I mean really drunk! For the life of me, I couldn't figure out how I went from casual drinking and drugs to being this wild party goer after I joined the church to help me change my life. The church people turned me out! We would go to the gay clubs on

Saturday night and then come to church on Sunday morning and serve in our various ministry areas.

I think what took me back to where I came from, the drugs and drinking, is the fact that I didn't have the right person to guide me as a new believer, to help shape my new life. As I think back, I don't believe I ever heard a sermon that made me want to turn my life around while I attended that church, and going out with choir members didn't make it any better. I believe I was just going to church because of my new friends. This behavior went on for years, even after I was married. Jonathan knew I was smoking, drinking, and going to clubs and would constantly pray for me to leave my old life behind and embrace the Christian life. I thought it was okay because "everyone else was doing it," even in other church ministries I encountered.

When the life of casual drinking and smoking was no longer enough, I got back into the hard stuff. I started snorting cocaine and drinking California Coolers every day. My cravings had gotten so bad that I sold the nice gold jewelry Jonathan worked so hard to buy me. At that point of my life, I wanted what I wanted and did what I wanted. I loved my angel so much, and he loved me the same. But I still wanted the other life, too; the one that appealed more to my flesh. I had yet to make a spiritual connection through the church. I had joined believing that I would be free from all my destructive habits, but the exact opposite happened. I thought I was leaving a world of drinking and drugs, but ended up going back to the same life. I didn't give much thought to what was happening in the church or what was happening to me. Even though I loved Jonathan, I was caught up in the worldly life again, and I wasn't ready to give it up. In fact, my life became worse than the one I had tried to escape. I played church for sixteen years from the time I joined the church in 1981 at twenty-one until 1997 well after we started our own church. Even though I had given God my

"Yes," to give Him my life in 1981, I didn't completely do so.

I also played at being a wife. We were newly married, and I didn't know the first thing about being married or a wife. We never had marriage counseling; we just wanted to be married. However, I still wanted to live how I was before I got married, so Jonathan and I had a lot of disagreements and arguments in our marriage. As a matter of fact, in the course of the first two years of our marriage, I left him about four times. I clearly lacked the understanding of "the two shall become one," (Genesis 2:24) and "if any man be in Christ he is a new creature, old things are passed away" (2 Corinthians 5:17).

Let me insert a bit of advice here. I don't recommend just getting married without going through marriage counseling first. Not saying that the person you're marrying is not the one for you, but it just helps the marriage if you talk about things with someone other than the two of you before you get married. The only marriage I had to model was my parents, and as you've read in the previous chapters, you see how that turned out. Jonathan had a better perspective of marriage than I did because his parents were good role models. It was great to have them as our example, even though they were not fond of our marriage because of the age difference and me having a child already. I knew he wanted our marriage to be great and to show his parents that he made the right choice when he married me, but unfortunately, in the beginning of our marriage, we had a lot of issues. Can you guess who was the cause of those issues? Me! I would say 95 percent of our issues came from me. The crazy thing is that all my family knew it was me. He was such a great guy, and to this day, he's even greater!

I even allowed *Eric* to creep back into my life. It wasn't because I wanted him to be a father to his son, but because he had all the drugs I needed. I wanted to be a good wife to the man of my dreams, but my addiction interfered with my ability to do so. My loving angel prayed for me continuously. I thank

God he kept praying and didn't give up on me even though I disappointed him time after time. He had the opportunity to be with a good, wholesome, well-groomed church girl, yet he chose me. It kind of reminds me of the story in the Bible about the Prophet Hosea who God told to marry the Prostitute Gomer (Hosea 1:2). I truly believe that God sent Jonathan Wade Allen to lead me to deliverance. I thank God for Jonathan's persistence in prayer and believing that God would deliver me from self-destruction.

I should have known that the time would come when I would reach the end of my rope and would no longer live the way I was living. It would've only been a matter of time before I would've had to surrender and let go. When that time came, I knew I wanted to give all of my addictions and bad behaviors to God and really get myself on the road to righteousness. But it didn't happen all at once; it was a process. Smoking was the first bad habit to go, and it wasn't even something I set out to do; it kind of just happened. I guess you could say it happened God's way!

My youngest son, Jonathan Jr., attended a Christian School in Upper Marlboro, Maryland. He would come home from school and read me the "rights of the Bible" from his school, and he would point out what I should and shouldn't be doing. He mainly referred to my smoking. My son came home daily with this one particular scripture, 1 Corinthians 6:19(KJV): "What? Know ye not that your body is the temple of the Holy Ghost which is in you, which ye have of God, and ye are not your own?" I wasn't paying that little boy no mind at all. When he would come to me, I would say to myself, *Boy, sit down somewhere*! But on one particular day, he came from school with the same scripture, and that time I wrote it down and stuck it in one of those small New Testament personal Bibles people used to hand out.

One day while at home, I was smoking like a chimney. I'd

probably smoked most of the pack before I started doing my hair that day. I usually smoked one cigarette after another while standing in the mirror doing my hair. On that day, all of a sudden, I had gotten tired of smoking. I stopped doing my hair and went to find that little small Bible with the piece of paper stuck in it. When I got the Bible, I began to read that scripture to the point where I just prayed and asked God to help me stop smoking. Instantly, I felt the taste of cigarettes leave me. I haven't had a cigarette in twenty-five years. Thanks be to God!

Drinking was also a major stronghold for me, and I knew that had to stop. I don't know if I drank because I liked the taste of alcohol or because it allowed me to escape my thoughts and problems. My drinking came to a head one night after I had gone to a club to support my sister-friend in a fashion show. I normally didn't drink dark liquor, but that night I did. I don't even know why. I had two drinks of dark Bacardi and coke. When it came time to leave, I was drunker than usual. I left the club and headed home. As I drove along the highway, I was so drunk and disoriented that I'd gotten myself lost. I didn't seem to remember where to get off the beltway at my exit. I drove up and down that beltway about three times before I finally took my exit for Landover. When I got home, I barely made it in the house. I rushed inside, headed right into the family room, and sat in the recliner because I was feeling sick to my stomach. It was so dumb of me to drink a liquor that I didn't usually drink. In that moment, in my drunken stupor, I prayed to God for deliverance. I prayed, "God, if you heal me this one time, I will never drink another drink." I believe that God heard me and responded because my sickness and drunkenness was gone immediately!

Once I was completely clean and sober, it dawned on me that God had been with me my whole life. In fact, He loved me so much that He didn't let me stay in the mess of a life that I had created for myself. Through His son Jesus, I became free, and God used my angel Jonathan to show me the way to salvation and forgiveness through Jesus Christ. Jonathan was consistent in his walk with Christ despite how I lived. He lived a life that witnessed to me not only Jonathan's love for me but also of God's amazing love for me.

Jonathan has been so amazing as we have walked through this whole process together. He stood by me when I was living in two different worlds, and he never forced me to choose because he had enough faith in God that I would be delivered. He continued to treat me like a queen even while I was still addicted to the things of the world. He prayed for me when *Eric* tried to draw me back into the drug scene. He stood with me as I battled fear and faced the changes that were necessary in order to move toward my God-given destiny. He stood for our marriage and our future when I really didn't believe I would make it through. Today, we minister to other married couples and give hope to those who feel they have done too much, sinned too greatly, or turned their backs on God one too many times.

Just as I recognized the way my parents lived in my childhood affected the choices I made in my life, I started to notice the exact same cycle taking place in my oldest son's life. I'm so grateful that I surrendered my life to God while our sons were young and that we worked hard to raise our children in a Christian home. Even though they were raised in the same environment, it's crazy to see how each of them chose their different paths. It was my prayer that they would both follow the same path of choosing Jesus. Unfortunately, Bootsy chose the streets, and Jonathan, Jr. chose the Savior. I can understand Bootsy's choice due to him living in two worlds between our home and his father's family home; he chose what appeared to him to be the better of the two. Bootsy lived with us during the week and spent most weekends with his grandmother on his father's side.

It was hard raising him in two homes with two different environments. Every Sunday when he returned home, we had to reteach him our house rules. We had to constantly remind him that what he was allowed to do at his grandmother's house wasn't allowed in our home. *Eric* was barely there when Bootsy went to visit his grandmother on weekends anyway. I am still very thankful to *Eric's* mother for allowing me to stay at her house during my troubled years, but that didn't mean that her lifestyle around my son was acceptable. I couldn't deny my son a relationship with his father or grandmother, but it was quite difficult to do so. Bootsy's grandmother and I stayed in touch occasionally as Bootsy got into his early teens and started getting in trouble with the law. Bootsy and his grandmother had a great relationship, and he loved her very much. Sadly, she died in 1990 when Bootsy was thirteen. I believe her death took a toll on him mentally, and it impacted him to the point where the streets were more appealing to him than the lifestyle of Christ I presented to him. And the fact that his father was from the streets and didn't care one way or another about the choices Bootsy made didn't make it any better.

Once we noticed the street life taking over Bootsy's life, we tried to help him by enrolling him in various youth programs and activities that would build a more solid foundation in his life and guide him in a more positive direction. Unfortunately, he made more poor choices by hanging out with the wrong crowd, stealing cars, and being arrested several times. Bootsy was caught up in the juvenile detention system from fourteen to seventeen years old. Between eighteen and forty-one, he served time in jail numerous times for distribution of narcotics and parole violations.

It's sad and unfortunate when parents don't see the potentially damaging effects their choices have on future generations. This is a cycle that has to be broken so that the next generations can be raised on solid foundations that will prepare them for their life's purpose as well as for living a life through the salvation of Jesus Christ. We must prevent our children from repeating the same mistakes we made so that their choices early in life won't have to be repaired due to the damage their bad decisions caused before they became mature adults. I was an absentee parent during Bootsy's formative years because I was so caught up in my own world. Even after I came out of the world, at the most critical time of my son's life, I allowed him, too, to live in two worlds, and he, unfortunately, chose the world I didn't want for him, repeating the cycle.

All parents need to look toward the future when they are making decisions to participate in non-productive, potentially destructive behavior for the sake of having fun, enjoying life, or doing what they want and realize the effect these choices will have on future generations. I sincerely pray that reading my story will help you to think about your own life choices.

Ephesians 4:22-24 (NKJV): *"That you put off, concerning your former conduct, the old man which grows corrupt according to the deceitful lusts, and be renewed in the spirit of your mind, and that you put on the new man which was created according to God, in true righteousness and holiness.*

We can't hold onto the old man and our former conduct and live for God at the same time. In order to live in true righteousness and holiness to God, we have to live fully and completely in the new man that we became when we gave our lives to Christ.

Reflection

Are there areas in your life where you are living in two worlds?

_____

_____

What are some things, relationships, habits, behaviors, thoughts, or mindsets that you need to let go of so that you can release and surrender yourself fully to God?

_____

_____

_____

_____

_____

_____

Can you honestly say that you fully trust God?

_____

_____

If you are living in two worlds and have some unsurrendered areas in your life, it's likely that you don't fully trust God.

Proverbs 3:5-10 (NLT): *"Trust in the Lord with all your heart; do not depend on your own understanding. Seek his will in all you do, and he will show you which path to take. Don't be impressed with your own wisdom. Instead, fear the Lord and turn away from evil. Then you will have healing for your body and strength for your bones. Honor the Lord with your wealth and with the best part of everything you produce. Then he will fill your barns with grain, and your vats will overflow with good wine."*

I admonish you to really give some thought to your life and how you're living. Evaluate every area of your life to see if it's fully submitted to God, and trust Him with everything and in everything. I can assure you that when you exchange your thoughts, ways, habits, etc. for God's thoughts, will, and purpose for your life, He promises to give you better than what you thought you had.

Concerning your Children

What are some things your child saw you do that you now wish you hadn't done, let alone in front of your child?

_____

_____

_____

Can you tell where those things affected or impacted your child and influenced some behaviors in them today?

_____

_____

_____

_____

_____

Did bad choices you made in your child's formative years have an impact on decisions they made as they got older?

_____

_____

_____

_____

_____

I encourage you to continue to pray for your children even in their adult years. Don't give up on them. Also, talk to your children and be honest with them about some wrong choices you've made in the past. If necessary, ask your children to forgive you for your shortcomings as a parent. Forgive your children for their faults as well, and together start with a clean slate and help guide them onto a better path.

7

Destined for Change

Not long after Jonathan and I were married, we moved outside of Greensboro, North Carolina. I was not at all happy about this move, and to show how disgruntled I was, I would travel just about every weekend to go back home to D.C. to visit my family. I was also determined to not have a "country" baby. My husband and I both grew up in the city, and I was determined that my child would be "a city kid" just like his parents.

It was a cold winter day in 1984, and my day was going well until my hubby came home from a very long day of school and work. He had worked both his shifts at his two jobs; he was a store manager at Wendy's and Bojangles while being a freshman in college. He and I got into an intense conversation because I wanted to go home to D.C. again for the weekend. He complained that I went home too much, and he argued that I needed to try and adjust to our new location and be there on

Sundays at the new church where he was being mentored. That conversation escalated into a huge argument, which gave me the excuse to hit the road.

As I headed to D.C. with Bootsy, I drove along listening to the radio. Later on, I asked him how he was feeling after the argument he witnessed; he said he was okay. After being on the road for several hours, my nerves were still bad from such an intense argument. At that point, the only thing that could've calmed me down was a cigarette. I tried not to smoke as much because of my pregnancy, but I reached for a cigarette from my purse anyway. I then tried to watch the road and look for the cigarette lighter socket in the middle of the console at the same time. I didn't do so well because I swerved off the highway. When I looked up from lighting my cigarette, my beautiful tan 1981 Volvo was doing a turbo ride up and down and in and out of a ditch. All I can remember is screaming, trying to grab a hold onto something in the car, and hoping my son was locked good into his seatbelt. I don't know if I called on the name of Jesus or was just screaming out. The impact of the crash threw me to the floor. When the car stopped, I quickly got up to make sure Bootsy was okay. I looked through the open space where the back window was and noticed car parts scattered all over the highway where the car hit a hole on the road. I sat in my car for a bit and looked around while I tried to calm my nerves. I noticed the cigarette lighter on the floor and picked it up to put it back in the socket.

I have absolutely no idea how we survived that, but I believe it was by the spirit of God. People had gotten out of their cars to help us out of our car, which was sitting in a ditch on three wheels. I never gave it much thought to realize how blessed I was to be alive, along with Bootsy and my unborn child. None of us were harmed in that accident. I wasn't in any pain, and I didn't have a scratch on me. Bootsy was just sitting in the back seat looking around. He wasn't crying and didn't have a scratch on him either.

I talked to the people around me like nothing had happened. When the state trooper came to the scene, he asked, "Whose car is this?" I'm sure he asked because he didn't see anyone in the car.

People responded, "It's hers," as if I did something wrong.

"Mines," I responded to the trooper in a low voice, slightly above a whisper while raising my hand.

With a look of disbelief on his face, he said, "I have never seen anything like this ever, and the person lived to tell about it."

It was so bad that the onlookers and the trooper asked me again if I was all right, and I assured them that I was. Following the accident, my pregnancy continued as expected for the remaining months, and I gave birth to Jonathan, Jr., who was a healthy baby with no abnormalities.

After we were helped out of the car, I had two different thoughts: My first thought was to call my husband, who I knew would come in a heartbeat to get his family. My second thought was to call my son's father, who I also knew would come in a heartbeat. *Eric* and I were still in communication with one another because of our son and the drugs I could still get from him. At the time of the accident, I was closer to Washington, D.C. where my dad lived than I was from where Jonathan and I lived in North Carolina. I chose to call *Eric* first, and he came to pick us up from the place where my car was towed in Richmond, VA. I was scared and alone, but I didn't call Jonathan and let him know what had happened. Even though I was shaken up from the accident, I was still mad about the fight we had, and I needed and wanted to get high; I knew I could do that with *Eric*.

I know you're probably thinking, drugs while pregnant? Yes, I was doing drugs while I was pregnant. I didn't know any better at the time. I eventually stopped doing cocaine because

I kept getting sick every time I tried to snort it. I guess that was my sign that I needed to stop. When *Eric* picked us up, he actually convinced me not to go home with him. As much as I wanted to go with him to get high, I listened and didn't go. He took Bootsy and me to my father's house instead. I eventually called Jonathan and told him all that had happened, and he came right away to get his family and take us back home. After that accident, I did some soul searching, and I realized that I just couldn't call another man to rescue me just because I got into a situation with my husband. I had a great husband who was a good father to my son, and he deserved better from me. Weeks later, we went and checked on my car where it had been towed. The auto collision company deemed my car repairable, which cost almost six thousand dollars in repairs with a five hundred dollar deductible.

After the accident, things with Jonathan and I started to get better. The accident caused Jonathan to see how important it was for me to be near my family, and he didn't want to risk anything else happening with me trying to make trips back and forth from North Carolina to D.C. He made it his mission to move me back to the D.C. area; I just had to be patient with the process.

In 1988, we bought our first home, a two-story townhouse in Landover, MD, from his oldest brother Joseph. It was a three-bedroom home with a fenced in backyard and two parking spaces. One of the perks was that we didn't have to cut the grass. It also had a connected living and dining room with a small kitchen. The kitchen was just the right size for a person who barely knew how to cook. As first-time homeowners, our home was perfect for us. The boys loved our new home, especially Bootsy because it wasn't in North Carolina. We lived in Landover for six years until we bought our first single family home in Ft. Washington, MD in 1994, where we still reside today. It's a big beautiful house. The previous owners were pastors who lived there for over thirty-five years. We didn't like the interior decor, so over the years, we've renovated the house to make it our own.

When you don't understand or know the grace you have been given by God, you take advantage of it and keep living life the way you want. The first car accident had shaken me up a bit, and I did get myself together afterward to do the best I could as a wife to my husband and a mother to my children. However, the lifestyle of partying, drinking, and drugs were also important to me, and I intertwined them trying to live in two worlds. After we were completely settled in Landover, I no longer had to travel the highway to get to what I needed or to do what I wanted. I loved hanging out with my two best friends Tammy and Terry, who were both single. They were the life of the party, and being with them helped me to escape my life as a wife, first lady, and mother, a life that I wasn't even sure I really wanted to be in at such a young age.

One day I went to the movies in Mazza Gallery in Northwest D.C. with my girls. Of course we didn't just watch a movie. Afterward, we hung out drinking as well. It was around 3:30 am when I left them and headed home to Landover, MD. I was on the I-495 beltway at exit 15 right before my exit at exit 17 Landover Road. I had slowed down on the highway because I was a little tipsy, and a car hit me from behind hard enough that it caused me to run into the car in front of me, which made that car run into the car in front of them. Wow, what a serious chain reaction! The car that hit me was associated with the people who I hit in front of me. When we got out of our cars to assess the damage, I noticed that they were just as drunk as I was. They were talking and just being crazy with one another. I hoped they wouldn't do anything to me because I was alone. All parties decided not to call the police to report anything because of the condition we were all in. We didn't need to take a breathalyzer test and risk getting arrested for driving under the influence. However, we exchanged driver's license and insurance information and took pictures of the damages.

I called Jonathan during the interaction to let him know what happened. He wanted to come get me, but I told him not to come since he had the boys, and he didn't need to bring them out for my foolishness. So we talked the entire time as I made the drive home. Unfortunately, I didn't walk away from this accident injury-free as I did with the first one. I incurred neck injuries and had to go to therapy for a while. But, luckily, I was able to collect the insurance money. Since I walked away from yet another accident, I questioned God as to why He kept sparing my life. What is so special about me that You keep protecting me?

As I was writing this, I thought to myself, What in the world were you thinking girl? A married woman with a great husband and two beautiful boys at home, and there you were hanging out like you had no responsibilities. I often ponder about how many married women would love to have a husband like mine, yet I acted like I didn't care one bit when he was so loving, caring, and understanding.

Last Chance

Even after the two accidents, I didn't recognize that God was using them to get my attention because I still hadn't totally committed my life to God. Even though I was reading the Bible, I wasn't applying the Word to my life as I needed to. I was just playing "preacher's wife" by showing up when I went to church or when my husband preached at different places. Even though I helped out, I really didn't want to be there. I was still smoking and drinking, not taking Christianity seriously.

Every weekend, my sisters, my brothers, and I used to take turns visiting one another's houses on the weekends. There was one sister's house where the family spent most of the weekends;

it was the gathering place. All the nieces, nephews, and friends of the family would be over there, even when family came to town. You could drink alcohol at all of my sisters' houses, but not at mine; my house was the least favorite to visit and still is to this day. When I traveled by myself, I didn't drink much, and if I did, it would be just a little to where it didn't affect my driving. I tried to do better. I knew that God wanted all of me, and it was past time for me to have given God all or nothing.

It was a fall day, and I was headed to my sister Carol's house in Takoma Park, MD. I was driving my beautiful, less than six-month-old, white 1989 Corsica. The roads were misty and slippery, which I didn't realize until my car began to slide on a curvy road. I lost control of the car, and there was nothing I could do. While gripping the steering wheel as tightly as I could, I closed my eyes and called out, "Jesus, Jesus, Jesus!" I don't know how many times I said Jesus, but all I know is that my car tumbled and tumbled and tumbled. The next thing I knew, my car came to a stop with me still in it. Praise God! My car had smashed through a gate and landed on top of a hill in someone's front yard. When I opened my eyes, broken glass from my front windshield was everywhere. I climbed out of my car the same way I did with the other accidents: like nothing happened. Once again, I survived a car accident without a scratch! Again, I didn't recognize that God had His hands on me and a hedge of protection around me.

Once I got my bearings, I called Jonathan, and he came right away as I knew he would. When he got there, the police and rescue unit were already there inspecting my car that was still sitting on top of the hill. My car was a wreck; it was damaged to the point where my axle was broken in half. The insurance company later declared it totaled. Many have lost their lives in car accidents where the car was totaled. I am so grateful that God saw fit, once again, to let me live to see another day. I see this accident as one God allowed to happen to stop me from going to the family gathering where I would've consumed alcohol and gotten behind the wheel inebriated. I believe God spared me this way so that I wouldn't destroy myself in a greater measure.

After that last traumatic experience, it started to sink in that God allowed me to survive another car accident. But why? I became more curious as to how I was able to walk away from such an accident that definitely should have killed me. I continuously asked God why He kept sparing my life. I was baffled to see that God wanted to save me when, based on my actions, I didn't deserve to be saved. That is the beauty of grace, God's undeserved and unmerited favor. God had a plan for me before I was born, and it was His will that His plan for me be fulfilled. What a merciful God!

After three accidents, I finally figured out that God was trying to get my attention. I started to understand years down the road why God would save someone with a history like mine. I didn't think anyone else other than my husband cared if I lived or died. They knew how reckless I had lived, and no one intervened. I didn't believe my friends cared about me because they never questioned the fact that I was a married pastor's wife who drank, did drugs, and hung out all hours of the night with them. I couldn't rely on or depend on anyone else to make a decision for me; I had to make the decision to change for myself, and I finally did.

There are many times on our life's journey when we come to a point where we're presented with the decision of which path we will take. We can choose the path of the Lord that will lead us to a life in Christ or the path of our flesh living a life of destruction, which in turn will lead us back to the decision of choosing Christ. It doesn't matter what road we choose in life because ultimately, all roads lead to Christ. It's just a matter of time before you choose Christ. If you choose a life away from him, it'll take you longer to get on the path of living for Christ, but eventually, any path you choose will always put you in a situation or circumstance that will present the life of Christ to you again and again.

That is exactly what happened to me with my three car accidents. Each accident presented me with the decision to turn away from the path of death and destruction that I was on, and each presented me with the opportunity to make the decision to change my life. In Deuteronomy 30:15-19, Moses gave a command from the Lord to the Israelites to make a choice about their lives once and for all. To choose whether they wanted life with blessings the Lord their God would give them or death and destruction by following after the gods of their ancestors. When I didn't make the right decision the first time (first accident), I was presented with a choice again (second accident). When I didn't make the decision of life that second time, I was presented with it yet again: the third accident. Although the third accident was greater than the first two, I thank God that I was unharmed and left in a sound state of mind where I was able to see that I had to choose the path of life; otherwise, there probably wouldn't have been another opportunity to make such a decision.

I want to encourage you to position yourself to where if you see people who are headed in the wrong direction, that you would share your decision to choose life to help steer them away from death and destruction.

Reflection

Can you recall a time or times in your life where you were presented with the opportunity to turn away from how you were living and choose a different path?

_____

_____

_____

_____

_____

_____

Did you make the right decision?

_____

_____

If no, why not?

_____

_____

_____

_____

If yes, what decision did you make and how did it impact your life from that point on?

_____

_____

_____

_____

_____

_____

_____

_____

_____

_____

_____

_____

_____

_____

_____

_____

_____

_____

8

My Evolution

Early in our marriage, Jonathan was awarded a football scholarship to Elon College in Burlington, North Carolina. During his first year at Elon College, he decided football was not what God had in mind for him, and he accepted his calling from the Lord to enter ministry. He committed his life to preaching the gospel at the age of eighteen. After serving for several years as a youth minister, Jonathan prayerfully and eagerly accepted his assignment from God to organize the Gospel Missionary Baptist Mission and the first worship service was held on Sunday, December 31, 1996. Later, we eventually transitioned from Gospel Missionary Baptist Mission to Gospel Missionary Baptist Church.

After the transition, people in the church began referring to me as First Lady, and I had absolutely no clue what that meant or how I was supposed to act. Even though I loved Jonathan and believed in what God had called him to do, I wasn't ready to be a pastor's wife. I barely knew how to be a mother, and I definitely didn't know how to be a wife let alone a first lady! I was confused about what I was supposed to do in the church because I didn't have a role model in my life to emulate as a first lady or minister's wife. From what I had seen, the first lady sat on the front row of the church in front of the pulpit, dressed beautifully, smiled, and shook hands with members of the congregation who greeted her. So, that's exactly what I did when we started our own church. It never dawned on me to ask the first lady of our old church if she would mentor me in my new role. Years later, people told me they thought I was stuck up. I really wasn't. I just wasn't comfortable being a first lady, and I had no idea how to connect with people. I was equally uncomfortable with the role since I was living in two worlds in the beginning and wasn't living my life fully committed to God.

After I got my life on the purposeful path living fully surrendered to God, He gave me His commission for my life, which was to preach and teach the gospel. As I grew in my relationship with God and learned the voice of the Holy Spirit, one day, I felt God tell me to write my testimony and share it with the ladies of our congregation. He directed me to Ruth 3:11 (KJV): "And now my daughter, fear not; I will do to thee all that thou requirest: for all the city of my people doth know that thou art a virtuous woman." My response to God was, "You have the wrong person." I didn't believe that I could do as God directed. I stuttered and had never been comfortable talking in front of people, and I was perfectly happy and content with being behind the scenes. I felt insecure about my speech impediment, and like Moses, I felt inadequate to fulfill God's plan for my life. However, just as God wouldn't allow Moses to escape his assignment, God wouldn't allow me to escape His call for my life either.

God allowed the events in my life to direct me to the

right path, and He also directed me towards working in my assignment and calling through various events that took place in my life. It seems as if God is kind of slick in how He directs our lives toward His path for us, but it's actually wonderful and truly amazing how He does it through how we generally navigate through life. I tried to convince God that He had made a mistake in wanting me to share my testimony, but I conceded because I've learned to obey whatever God tells me to do. So, I wrote out several pages of testimony and prepared to give my testimony at the next women's gathering.

While I was speaking at the gathering, I ended up sharing my entire story with the women. When I finished, there was not a dry eye in the place. I was so glad I obeyed the Lord. I felt as if the ladies of the church were now able to connect to me, understand where I'd come from, and know why I shied away from physical contact. Sharing my story has had a tremendous impact on my life, and I know it will have the power to help others to follow and live for Christ too.

While in New Orleans at the 1997 Essence Jazz Festival listening to the preachings of some powerful and anointed women, I felt the Holy Spirit tell me I was called to preach. I didn't know how to process what I was sensing in my spirit, especially since my husband and I came from a church background that didn't believe in women preachers. I felt insecure about who I was and what I was supposed to do for God because of my past and the way many in that first church had treated me. However, I had given my life to God and learned to listen to the voice of His Holy Spirit. God even directed me toward higher education even though I didn't even have a high school diploma, but I knew I had to trust that He had a greater purpose for me and my life.

I had a major wake-up call while trying to help Jonathan Jr. with his math homework. It was quite depressing not being able to help my child with his school work because I had cut my own education short. So, in 2000, at the age of forty, I made the decision to obtain my GED. It was another step I made toward changing my life for the better so that I could get a higher education and prepare for ministry as the Lord directed. I completed the necessary classes and tests, and I was awarded my GED in 2000.

When the Lord told me to go to Bible College next, I didn't waste any time. I went to the college to meet with the administrator, and I discovered that classes had already been in session for a month. She advised me to wait for the next semester because a lot of material had already been covered, and I would have a lot of work to make up. I didn't want to delay and was eager to move into the role God had called me to. Not one to back down from a challenge and knowing the Lord told me to do this, I asked her what I would have to do to get caught up. She shook her head like she didn't believe I could do it, but she allowed me to enroll in the class and told me I would need to meet with the instructor before class to get all of the assignments. I attended class, got the missed assignments, went home that week, did all of the previously missed homework, and turned in my work the following Saturday before class. I never missed a class. I attended Bible College for four years and graduated in June 2004. What seems impossible to man is possible with God. Not only did I graduate, but I was valedictorian of my class. I was told that the valedictorian had to give a seven-minute speech at the graduation ceremony. Even though I feared I would stutter my way through the entire seven minutes, I gave the speech anyway.

Following graduation, I asked my husband what I was supposed to do with all the information I learned from Bible College. He said I should teach children and women. Now, I know what the Lord had told me about preaching, and I didn't want to settle for doing anything less than what He told me to do. So I gathered some other women around me, and we prayed that my husband would be delivered from that false belief about women preachers. The Lord began to convict him about his beliefs, and one day he came to me and asked me to write out what I believed the Lord had called me to do with all the biblical information I learned in college. I was honest with him and wrote about how the Lord told me through His Holy Spirit that I was called to teach and preach. After reviewing what I'd written, he agreed to allow me to become a minister in the church.

On Sunday, April 29, 2007, I preached my initial sermon titled "Double Dipping" with Romans 12:2 as my foundational scripture. I was then licensed as a minister to preach the Gospel. I was so excited that my pastor, my husband, licensed me. At that time, our church was the Gospel Church, and we were renting a school auditorium in Temple Hills, MD called J. Frank Dent to hold our Sunday morning services. The week leading up to this life-changing event for me, I received calls from so many people checking on me or asking if I needed anything. That entire week, I kept asking God for confirmation that this was what He really wanted me to do. I also asked my husband why I needed to go through all that initial sermon stuff because I believed it was just for man to see. My husband responded that it was the protocol in case you were invited to preach at a church, and they wanted proof of your calling. I accepted what he said even though preaching a sermon is not proof of a calling.

On the day of my sermon, I wore a pink two-piece cape and skirt I'd made that week. I had to look my best. My co-workers, friends from out of town, and friends from other churches came to attend this momentous occasion. If I didn't know any better, I would've thought all of Maryland was present. At least that's how it looked from where I was sitting. The school auditorium held over two hundred people, and it was filled to capacity and overflow. My husband helped me work on my sermon, but I was anxious to get it over with. The service started, and the program went as scheduled. When I got up to preach, I was a nervous wreck. I started with my opening and preached from my notes. I thought it went real fast, and I didn't think I did a good job because I was so nervous. At the end of service, many people came to congratulate me. Of course it went in one ear and right out the other because I didn't believe in myself at that time the way that I do today.

After getting licensed, I didn't want to stop there. Once again, I talked to my pastor about the idea of me being ordained. Although I observed that it was all about man, I shared with him my thoughts on the matter and why I felt I should be ordained. I explained that I had been sitting and training under him for ten years, and he had seen me wear many hats and oversee several ministries in the church. I gave him the rundown of all that I'd been doing the last ten years, such as women's ministry, children's ministry, ushering, teaching bible study, and facilitating meetings. He agreed with my thoughts and decided to do ordination his way, not the traditional way.

Our ministry was expanding, and we wanted a location of our own. After searching extensively, we finally found a location about ten minutes from the school we rented. On Sunday March 7, 2010 in our new location, I was ordained as an Associate Pastor of our ministry. I was ordained along with three other members who were being commissioned for their callings. After the Ordination and Commissioning service, I was honored to serve in the position alongside my husband. I was also so relieved that I didn't have to preach a sermon this time around to be ordained. I was truly thankful for the way my husband performed the ordination because I remembered all he had to go through when he was ordained.

After I completed my Christian education and was ordained, I was ready to move into the next phase God had for me. I felt like I had a lot of ground to cover and had to make up for so many wasted years. I went on to college to study for my bachelor's degree. I received a Bachelor of Arts in Biblical Studies, Church Organization, and Management from Azusa World Ministry Training Institute in Phoenix, Arizona in June 2011. I am currently working on my master's degree at Virginia Union University.

When I dated a drug dealer and sold drugs, I lived a good life and had some of the best things money could buy. After committing to a Christian lifestyle, I didn't believe that I could still have the best life had to offer. I now know that God wanted me to experience the good life and show that His way of prospering me was better than that of the streets. I now own three successful businesses, one of which I own with my husband. From all I have accomplished over the years, the saying, "It's not how you start, but how you finish," certainly rings true concerning me. After reading the story of the beginning of my life and all that I've done and experienced, would you have guessed that I'd accomplish all that I have?

If God can transform a wounded girl like me, who had a very broken and sordid past, He can transform anyone. If your life is not where it should be at this point, don't discredit it. Know that God's will, purpose, and plan for your life can be fulfilled in the earth if you surrender your life to Him and follow His plan for you. Your life is not too far gone, and your past is not too dark for God to use it for His glory. The tribulations you have overcome are what God will use to make an impact on the lives of others who you will eventually come in contact with. He will also use your story to inspire others to not give up or quit and know that there is a purpose and plan for their lives too. I encourage you to seek His guidance and trust He will give you whatever you need to fulfill the purpose and destiny He has placed within you.

As I look back over my life, I am continuously amazed at the great work God has done in me and through me. Because of my own amazing testimony, I have learned to not give up on people who live on the wrong path. God is rich in grace and mercy, and I know that if He can save and deliver me from my life of death and destruction to put me on the right path to my destiny, then he can do the same for anyone. I thank God for my deliverance and for every opportunity when I get to share with others and give them hope and encouragement that life can get better regardless of how it started.

Even after living life as a Christian, you will experience trials and tribulations. But storms don't last always, and situations do get better. You have to keep your focus on God, stay in His word, and remember the scripture in Romans 8:28 (KJV): "And we know that all things work together for good of them that love God, to them who are the called according to His purpose." You are still alive, and you didn't die from your past or destructive behaviors because God has a purpose and plan for your life here on earth. Be encouraged and seek the Lord in what He wants to do in you and through you to bring forth His glory.

Now unto Him who is able to do exceedingly abundantly above all that we ask or think according to the power that works in us (Ephesians 3:20).

Where a person's life starts out doesn't mean that's where it will be forever or if that's how it's going to end. I am living proof of this. Reading my story, you would think I was a hopeless case. I, too, would have had pity on me and seen me as a hopeless case. My life had gotten worse, which led me to want nothing to do with the destructive lifestyle I had been living. I eventually made it down a path that led me to God's divine will and purpose for my life.

We really and truly do not have to stay at the same place or level in which we started. Your current situation is not and does not have to be your final destination. There is always room for growth, and we should be growing in every area of our lives. As a matter of fact, you evolve without even trying. Think back to when you were a kid and you were asked what you want to be when you grow up. Are you where you said you wanted to be as an adult? Not everyone becomes what they said they wanted to do as a child. Even some people who did follow the path to become what they dreamed of being often have changed their minds and became or did something different later in life. Once again, the way our lives start is not always how it will end. As a matter of fact, we have seen far too many people in the world who grew up in extreme poverty to become successful business people and millionaires.

Reflection

Do you see any areas in your life where you need to change so that you can evolve?

_____

_____

_____

Do you know what it is that God wants you to do in your life?

_____

_____

_____

Are you doing it?

_____

If so, I applaud you. What did it take for you to evolve into God's purpose and plan for your life?

_____

_____

_____

_____

Are there additional things you feel you can do to take it to the next level?

_____

_____

_____

_____

If not, identify areas or people in your life that may be holding you back. What do you need to do to move into God's purpose and plan for you?

_____

_____

_____

_____

_____

_____

_____

_____

_____

_____

_____

Last Words

As hard as it was for me to write my story for the world to read, I did so because it is what God wanted me to do. There is power in my story. Power to inspire, power to impact, and power to impart. As you read my story, I pray that you were inspired by my journey and saw that I didn't become a casualty to my situation or circumstance because I rose above them to become and live in God's purpose for me and who He called me to be.

I pray that you were inspired to not let your past dictate your future just as I didn't let my past dictate my future. I pray that my story made some form of impact on you to know that it's not how you start, but it's how you finish. I pray that you will look forward to your destiny that is before you and run with purpose because life is not over for you yet. It begins exactly where and when you make the decision to start. I pray that you were imparted with the spirit of the message God wanted you to receive through my story and the scriptures that were related throughout the reading. I pray that as you were reading my story, reading the life lessons, and doing the reflection exercises that you examined your life and came to know that you, too, are destined for change.

About the Author

Pastor Kimberly R. Allen, affectionately known as Lady Kim is a native of Washington, D.C. She is an Associate Pastor of Connect Church in Waldorf, MD, founded and pastored by her husband, Jonathan W. Allen, Sr.

Pastor Kim has been married to Pastor Jonathan for thirty-35 years. They have two sons, James R. Reeder and Jonathan W. Allen, Jr.; one grandson, Jaquan McShay; and one granddaughter, Iyana Reeder.

Pastor Kim leads the church's Women's Ministry and is also Coordinator for New Members Class, Connect 12 Ministry, and Greeters ministry. Pastors Jonathan and Kim are co-labors of Couples Strengthening Couples, a marriage ministry that has hosted married couples every 4th Sunday at their home for the last six years. Pastor Kim gives all honor and praise to God for what He has allowed her to do and be in this life.

A firm believer in "obedience births blessing," Pastor Kim obtained her GED in 2000 at the age 40, after dropping out of

High School at the age of seventeen. She went on to graduate from Given's Bible College in June 2004 as Valedictorian of her class. She then earned her Bachelor's Degree in Biblical Studies, Church Organization and Management from Azusa World Ministry Training Institute in Phoenix, Arizona, under the direction of Drs. Alfred and Beverly Craig, in June 2010. Pastor Kim is currently a senior at Virginia Union University and is expected to graduate in May 2021 earning her Masters of Divinity.

Pastor Kim is a business owner of Finally Talls By KYRA, fashions made for the 21st century tall women. She is also the owner of God's Hot Off The Press Production, specializing in mass T-shirt production, where design and print come together. Pastor Kim, also owns and operates a tuition-free Christian summer camp since 2002.

Living in Two Worlds - Destined for Change, a memoir about her life is Pastor Kim's first book, published by Allen Ministries Publishing Company.

Made in the USA
Middletown, DE
16 May 2021